Overleaf: Designed for Mrs Cuming, this pool has a characteristic simple stone edging and masses of erigeron

EDNA WALLING
AND HER GARDENS

SECOND EDITION

PETER WATTS

FLORILEGIUM

For Jo, William, Alistair and Harriet

The author and publisher would like to thank the following for
permission to reproduce photographs: Jenny Churchill — cover,
pp2, 19, 37, 41, 45, 49, 53, 56, 59, 71, 73, 76, 84, 88, 101,
109, 112, 117; Richard Stringer — pp66, 67, 120; Mark Strizic —
pp83, 111; Mrs Elisabeth Morson — pp85, 86, 87, 114.

Cover photograph by Jennie Churchill:
Edna Walling designed this cottage and garden, Downderry, for her mother.
It was one of the first cottages at Bickleigh Vale.

First published as *The Gardens of Edna Walling* in 1981
by the Women's Committee of the
National Trust of Australia (Victoria)
Reprinted 1982

Second edition published in 1991 by Florilegium
Reprinted 1997   2nd reprint 2002

Copyright © Peter Watts 1991

National Library of Australia
Cataloguing in Publication data:
Watts, Peter, 1949–
    Edna Walling and her gardens.

    2nd ed.
    Bibliography.
    Includes index.
    ISBN 0 646 04466 4.

    1. Walling, Edna, 1896–1973. 2. Landscape gardening
    – Australia – History. 3. Gardens – Australia –
    History. I. Watts, Peter, 1949–   . Gardens of
    Edna Walling. II. Title. III. Title: The gardens of
    Edna Walling.

712. 6092

Set in Palatino by Meredith Typesetters, Melbourne and Netan Pty Limited, Sydney
Printed by Kyodo Printing Co. Pte Ltd

CONTENTS

PREFACE

It is ten years since this book was first published, and since that time Edna Walling has assumed almost cult status. Some of her books have been republished; her unpublished writings and photographs have been dusted off and given a public airing; and many of her surviving gardens have been documented in other books. In that short ten years there have also been numerous books, articles, radio and television programs devoted to her work. Regrettably, no one has chosen to 'fill out' the biography and analysis of her work attempted here in 1981. This book has been unavailable for many years and I am delighted that Gilbert Teague and his Florilegium should choose to republish it.

Since the time this book was first published Anne Latreille's excellent biography of Ellis Stones and a great many articles and books have helped place the work of Edna Walling in a much better context. More work remains — especially about the careers of Edna's contemporaries, such as Olive Mellor and Milly Gibson, and then later Mervyn Davis and Beryl Mann, amongst others. No doubt more information will come to light as the interest in Australia's garden history grows.

In this new edition there are many new photographs, minor alterations to the text and an updated bibliography.

PREFACE TO FIRST EDITION

As a woman who worked prodigiously in many different fields, Edna Walling left behind an enormous web of threads for a would-be biographer to untangle. Indeed so wide is her network of surviving acquaintances, photographs, gardens and writings that it would have taken several years of full-time labour to follow all these trails to their end. Regrettably, this time was not available to me, and this is not the book I really wanted to write. I would have preferred to give a much longer and more detailed account of her life. But I decided, nevertheless, that the material collected over the past five years — especially the exquisite water-colour sketches done by Edna Walling — was of sufficient interest to publish.

In many ways Edna Walling was a public figure. But at the same time she retained an elusive and enigmatic quality. If this book helps to reveal her more fully, and establish the important place she holds in Australian garden history, then it will not have been without purpose.

There are many people who have assisted with the research for and production of this book. I owe a special debt of gratitude to David Yencken who, probably unknowingly — or perhaps cunningly — has urged me on when often my energy was flagging. Warwick and Suzie Forge have also provided much-needed support and advice.

I am especially grateful to Joan Law-Smith for providing such a delightful foreword and to Edna Walling's niece, Barbara Barnes, for making available many unpublished notes and manuscripts. My thanks must also go to Jim Willis for checking and updating the list of plants.

There are many others who have helped in a variety of ways; with some I have enjoyed many pleasurable hours talking and roaming around the most enchanting gardens. I am particularly indebted to Eric Hammond, the late Lorna Fielden, Jean Galbraith, Brian and Jan McKeever, Glen Wilson, the late Ellis Stones, Mr and Mrs Frank Walker, Mervyn Davis, Daphne Pearson, Grace Fraser, Joan Jones, Anne Latreille, Rob and Jane de Caen, Olive Mellor, Beryl Wilson, Geoff and Sharyn Nixon, Howard Tanner, Gwynnyth Taylor, the late Leonard Cox, and Blanche Marshall. I am grateful to owners of drawings reproduced and gardens illustrated. Brian and Jan McKeever, Glen Wilson, Mr and Mrs Frank Walker, Beryl Wilson and Blanche Marshall have already been mentioned. I must also thank Andrew and Sue Manifold, Dean Nelson, the Cairnmillar Institute, Mrs I. D. McKinnon, Rodger and Gwen Elliot, W. F. Grassick, Barbara Wehner, Alison Balfour, Mr and Mrs Laurie Ledger, the Lady Vestey, Jim Beattie, Sir Roderick and Lady Carnegie, Mr and Mrs John Cook, and Mr and Mrs Dudley Cain.

It has been a great pleasure to work with the talented and dedicated group of people who produced this book. Their attention to quality and detail has, I hope, made up for my own inadequacies. Margaret Darling, the President of the National Trust in Victoria, was immediately enthusiastic when we first discussed the book and has carefully guided its development; Margaret Barrett has had the unenviable task, performed with great patience and tact, of editing my often illegible handwriting into a readable text; Barbara Martella, who typed the manuscript, is accustomed to deciphering that handwriting!

I take this opportunity of offering my sincere thanks to the hardworking Women's Committee of the National Trust of Australia (Victoria) for giving me the opportunity to unburden my thoughts on Edna Walling, and to the Council of the National Trust for allowing me to foster a growing interest in historic gardens generally.

And lastly I thank my wife, Jo, who has so patiently allowed me to have 'another woman' in my life.

P.W.

1981

FOREWORD

The happiest events in our lives are often carefully preserved in memory as acts of providence. A chance meeting or experience, or the guidance of an inspired teacher, may open a door to deeper insights, undreamed-of discoveries.

Long ago, when I was about ten years of age, such a door was opened for me. It would be more appropriate in this instance to say 'a gate', because I met Edna Walling when she came to design part of my parents' garden. While I recognised at that early age, albeit dreamily, the beauty of plants and trees, I had never before met a person who could take the materials of the earth — the living things, the stones and the water — and plant and construct them to form a garden.

I retain a vivid recollection of our gardener's almost apoplectic reaction to Edna Walling on that first day. As though it was not enough for him to be faced with a woman whose directions he would have to follow — bless his very masculine heart — she had the presumption to wear a man's clothing! Also his ideals of beauty, where gardening was concerned, were very large mauve dahlias: so you see there was no common ground, aesthetically speaking, on which they could meet.

So there she was, dressed in her jodhpurs and shirt: the sensible shoes, the closely cropped hair, bleached by the sun. There were no signs of personal vanity that might cause a moment's interruption to the task in hand: no wayward lock of hair to be swept from her eyes, her hat temporarily laid aside — or perhaps it had been swept off by the wind. She went about her work with a never-to-be-forgotten sense of purpose.

I can remember wondering, as the transformation of our garden proceeded, why she should choose to plant such a dull affair as the Russian olive beneath a walk of fairly mature silver poplars. Many years were to pass, and I was to make many mistakes, before I recognised the wisdom of her decision. Apart from learning that few other plants would have the tenacity to grow in competition with such established neighbours, I came in time to observe that on a windy day the under-sides of the *Elaeagnus* leaves were a subtle echo of the silver leaves above. Thus the affection I had for Edna Walling grew into esteem.

Some plants of opposing hemispheres and climates are obviously ill at ease in each other's company. Edna Walling knew which species of tree or shrub to place alongside another, and what plants would be in sympathy growing beneath. Her combination of forms, textures and colours, her abhorrence of anything contrived or vulgar (such as the use of 'purple-leaved wonders'), and her discretion in avoiding violent contrasts that can occur with highly coloured or variegated foliage plants or trees: all this garden wisdom contributed to the sense of serenity that was so impressive in her work.

Edna Walling was an artist, and also something much more, a creator of harmony. She was not a writer of music in the strictly aural sense, using those notes of melodic progression hovering above, within and beneath the five stave lines. It was another kind of music she composed: just such a magical procession, but using earth's bounty as her source of inspiration — a harmony not for the ears but for the eyes, the mind and the spirit. It is a harmony that we find too in her delicately executed and clearly informative plans.

A garden to her was a *happening,* an echo of a woodland, containing the same qualities of mystery and peace, but it was also a place where compromises had to be made, because human beings as well as birds and animals had to live within its boundaries. Certain plants that she especially loved became a *leitmotiv* in her work, as notes of colour or form where she needed them, but never repeated in such a way as to be monotonous. I cannot walk past *Erigeron karvinskianus* in our garden without thinking of her; evocative too are her beloved Westmoreland thyme and the low-growing campanulas mentioned often in her writings.

Edna Walling's concern also embraced the world beyond the garden. In *The Australian Roadside* she begins by saying: 'The thought of any journey to a place where the trees and natural ground cover are still unspoilt is thrilling to me.' These words lead us into a book of wide ecological knowledge, the characteristics and qualities of the Australian countryside being observed and noted with the approach of a true landscape architect — one who believes in conserving and, if necessary, recreating the natural scene in its original beauty, with its trees, shrubs, flowers and grasses all interdependent in their existence together.

It is a matter of profound regret to me that so often people who have a clear vision and a dedication to a certain ideal for the benefit of humanity are not always appreciated in their lifetime. During Edna Walling's life she seemed to be working and writing in a wilderness of indifference to the environment as a whole. It must have been heartbreaking, at times beyond endurance, for a person who was so aware of the tragedy and finality of thoughtless destruction.

It is with gratitude to Peter Watts that I have read this biography; and it is a tribute to his sensibility that he should have chosen to write it. It has obviously been a labour of love — but a labour nevertheless. It has entailed much painstaking work to visit gardens, research the designer's writings, and trace many details to give a more complete picture of Edna Walling's life and work as it evolved from her early formative years. This is an inspiring story, and the chapter entitled 'The Legacies of Edna Walling' is of special significance because here the author sums up so perceptively that wisdom of which we are the fortunate beneficiaries.

Let us take her lessons to heart and cherish the memory of a very rare individual who cared enough for humanity and nature to unite them in a deeper understanding.

Joan Law-Smith
1981

CHAPTER ONE:
FROM BICKLEIGH
TO BENDLES

'My father thought I would be a boy (he had one girl so why not!) and he went right ahead with his preconceived ideas on "how to bring a boy up hardy"; in spite of the turn of events he went straight ahead . . . I was sent to the best school in Plymouth (not Father's idea, he could think of lots of better ways of spending money than that. He would buy me some tools and set me to work on making something). They weren't at all nice to me at this school; they just couldn't stand that stupid little red-headed girl who never would be able to remember 1066 and all that.'

So wrote Edna Walling in an unpublished article she variously called 'My Mother and Father', 'Life', 'So there it was', and finally 'As Far Back as I can Remember'. From a 'stupid little red-headed girl' in Bickleigh, near Plymouth, England, she grew to be one of the most influential garden designers and conservationists in far-away Australia.

Edna Margaret Walling was born in Yorkshire on 4 December 1896, the second daughter of William and Margaret Walling. It was around Plymouth in Devon, however, that the young Edna spent her early years. Her father was engaged in

Downderry, Bickleigh Vale village, soon after its completion and well before its garden had reached maturity

a business that yielded a comfortable though not extravagant living. Bitterly disappointed that his second child was also a girl, he was determined 'to make a man of this little girl; always forgetting she wasn't a little boy'. So while her elder sister Doris was busy playing with dolls, Edna would be making a new bow and arrow or engaged in her 'sculpturing activities', which turned part of the back garden of their terrace house into 'exciting little mountains and low spreading meadows, and streams and lakes'. Even at this stage in her life, 'Earth to me was something to mould, not grow things in — plants got in the way of my sculpturing. . . '

The Walling family was not exceptional in any way. Both parents sang in the choir at St Andrews Cathedral. They would often take one of the small rowing boats in Plymouth Sound, and sometimes, with picnic basket aboard, would row to Mount Edgaimbe. They would visit the Barbican to watch the fishing smacks sail in, or go to Plym Bridge 'where the bluebells grew in huge carpets, and the foxgloves waved gently amongst the birches, and the lovely old stone bridge imprinted itself on my mind so indelibly that to this day I long to build one'. They also regularly attended orchestral concerts at the Plymouth Guildhall. It was while returning from one of these concerts that, from the top of a double-decker tram, the family saw William Walling's business premises entirely enveloped in flames. Edna later remembered 'feeling so important that it was *our* store that was burnt down and causing such a stir' — such is the joyous irresponsibility of childhood. Her emotions must have been quite different when, thirty years later, she stood helplessly by as her own house, with all its precious contents, burnt to the ground.

The loss of the uninsured Walling business was, in fact, a family catastrophe. Edna had to leave 'the best school in Plymouth', though to her it was 'a glorious escape'. Soon after this, however, she suffered a serious bout of pneumonia. For six weeks she lay between life and death, constantly nursed by her mother during the day and by her father at night. As she slowly began to recover, her father taught her to play a flageolet, a small wind instrument, to encourage her to breathe more deeply. These lessons stayed with her all her life; from this little bone instrument she graduated to a recorder, which she played intermittently for many years. As her strength gradually returned she was permitted occasionally to accompany her doctor on his rounds. She sat proudly in the brougham next to the doctor in his tall silk hat, with the coachman, also silk-hatted, up on his top seat.

Between-times private lessons were taken with a neighbour, and eventually Edna was enrolled at a new school in Plymouth, the Convent of Notre Dame. She later recalled that the sisters 'soon discovered the weak points and looked around for something to work on; they helped me over history and English so that I wouldn't make too shocking an exhibition in my reports, and encouraged the tendency towards drawing and geometry, for which I shall everlastingly love them'.

Despite all the problems with school, sickness and the loss of the family's business, these were blissful years for the young Edna. She was devoted to her family. Having taught her the woodworking skills, her father maintained a list of items for her to mend or make — pictures to be framed, shelves to be put up and painted. Although she liked making things, she preferred them to be of her own choosing. She was delighted, therefore, when a judge at the local Art and Crafts Show branded one of her articles 'pernickety in the extreme'. This wounded her father's pride, however, and soon put a stop to his job-listing.

But the activities of these early years that Edna enjoyed most, and which clearly left a distinct impression on her mind, were those associated with the Devonshire countryside. It was not unusual for father and daughter to walk up to twenty miles at one stretch across the moors. Edna herself attributed to these walks her 'intense love of low-growing plants, of mauves and soft greens, of mossy boulders and gritty pathways and closely nibbled turf'. This, she said, was 'the type of garden I love best'. Together they admired, too, the simple stone cottages with their intimate gardens. Her father had little interest in plant life on these walks but enjoyed playing guessing games such as 'how far it was to that stunted tree, how much fall there was in the ground to that large boulder, how high was that stone wall and how many feet wide'. These games amounted, of course, to highly palatable lessons in perspective.

When Edna was fourteen the family decided to leave England. It was a sad departure, for by this time Edna had at last come to enjoy school, having developed a deep affection for some of the staff and her fellow pupils. There was some talk of her staying on. The Mother Superior tried to persuade Mrs Walling to leave her younger daughter, but in the end Edna herself decided that she could not bear the thought of parting with her family. When she left England, however, Edna had already absorbed many of the influences that were to direct her life. For the next six years they lay dormant, until the right opportunity presented itself and launched her upon her career.

In November 1911 the family set sail on the *Aeawa* for New Zealand, where William Walling had a contract with the Hutchinson Scales Company. The Wallings were not especially happy in their new home. Edna longed for her friends, a longing that became intolerable at times. It was possibly her enjoyment of the countryside that led her to take a position on a country station at Kituna, where she cooked (something that never gave her any pleasure) and cleaned. 'Twelve months in such a job was an education in itself but it was considered sufficient and I was brought back to the "refinement" of the family circle once again.' By this time William Walling had already departed for Australia, where he became warehouse director with Toledo Berkel. While the family waited for word to join him, Edna began to train as a nurse in a Christchurch private hospital. It was a surprising and uncharacteristic move, and even more surprisingly she enjoyed nursing and thought of staying on when her mother moved to Melbourne after six months. But it was her father's reminder of the open-air life she was forgoing that persuaded her to give up the position. They settled into the new house, 'Arundel', in Commercial Road, South Yarra, and

Boredom of idleness drove me off in search of 'my life's work'. Many were the fruitless avenues Mother and I explored before we hit upon the School of Horticulture and I remember so clearly the dampening effect the principal's question 'Is she artistic?' had upon me. That's the last thing I was, I felt. Mother's 'Oh, yes' sounded most emphatic and sincere but I feared 'twas but Mother love. She had said things about my being a landscape gardener to the principal though I never remember the slightest discussion upon the subject before we entered that room — whether she had just thought of it or whether she had it in her mind for some time subconsciously I never knew — at all events the idea did not sink into my consciousness even then or for some time to come. All I longed for was the soil: what I was to do with it wasn't clear, nor did it bother me. Being enrolled at this school I came closer to it than I had ever been before and that was all that mattered for the time being.

Edna Walling commenced the full-time course at Burnley Horticultural College on 4 September 1916 at the age of nineteen. She attended for the whole of 1917 and was awarded certificate number 44. Examination records for 1917 show her performance to have been among the best in her class. Comments in the record include 'a very fine student, making excellent progress'; 'alert and hard-working student,

Downderry today is the epitome of the cottage style

examination results very good'. The full-time certificate course comprised about half practical horticulture and half classwork on ornamentals, fruit, vegetables, landscape design and sciences relating to horticulture. Despite her good results Edna herself thought she

showed no particular promise beyond a capacity for the most laborious tasks. I took inordinate delight in such jobs as wheeling a mound of soil from one spot to another — in digging the strips of soil between the trees in the orchard — in fact anything that was straight forward and somewhat bullocking in nature. I found the few lectures on landscape gardening boring and the lessons on design which were to help us with the drawing of plans extremely tedious. I obtained 99 per cent for fruit canning, the announcement of which was greeted by an uproarious 'that was because you were so good at soldering the tops'.

In fact, she noted in the foreword of her first book, *Gardens in Australia*, that her time at Burnley was 'a . . . course of insubordination, fittingly brought to a close with an illuminated certificate which magnificently refrained from telling the world all that I did not know!'

By her twenty-first birthday in December 1917 Edna had that certificate, 'but no set course in life'. She felt impelled now to make her own way, and so decided to do jobbing gardening. She recalled later that she was appreciated for her straight eye, her tidiness and her strength. The last quality, as her unpublished notes reveal, 'meant that they could order me to wheel in the manure from the footpath without worrying whether it would kill me'. During these two years of hard physical labour she developed a hatred for gardens that 'grew deeper and deeper'.

It was the sight of a stone wall supporting a semi-circular terrace that was her salvation. As soon as she saw it, about 1919, her approach to gardens changed: 'From then on, gardens for me became a chance to carry out the architectural designs in my head instead of places where one slaved for too many hours of the precious days.' An architect brother of one of her gardening colleagues willingly gave her the opportunity to design the garden of a house he was building. And so it began. Further gardens were required for this architect, then for others, until the public, or at least the wealthier sections of it, insisted that Walling, and no other, design their gardens. In these formative years she recognised that 'father's training was now bearing fruit. "How far is it to that tree? How high is that wall?" became of vital concern'.

Edna (in the hat) among her fellow students at Burnley Horticultural College

Throughout her life Edna Walling was a keen naturalist, and in these early years she had ample time for camping and walking in the bush. It was during one of these walking expeditions with her friend Eileen Bamford, another ex-Burnley student, that she came across a 'For Sale' sign on a piece of land at Mooroolbark, east of Melbourne. She wanted that land instantly. It comprised 3 acres of rolling farmland at the foot of Mount Dandenong, on which grew what she later called 'a few rather depressing she-oaks', trees that her mother considered to be attractive right from the start. With a deposit of £5 that piece of land was secured. The title is dated 1927 and made out in the name of 'Edna Margaret Walling. Occupation — Garden Architect'. ('Garden Architect' was not Edna's usual term — for most of her life she called herself a landscape designer, and never a landscape architect.) Despite the date marked on the title, Edna was in residence well before 1927 and probably her first building was completed by the end of 1921.

Having felt the urge to acquire the land as 'a sort of mooring, an experimental ground, and my own roof', Edna was also able to put into practice an idea she had been mulling over for a year or two. She wanted to prove it was possible to build a cottage of charm and personality that pleased the eye and cost no more than a

conventional house. And this she set about doing. A nearby excavation provided stone for the floor, walls and chimney; packing cases from her father's factory made cheap and handsome internal lining boards; malthion was scrounged for the roof; and saplings cut from the site provided an attractive and functional pergola. In *The Australia Handbook*, a booklet published by the Australia Hotel, Walling described the building of this first cottage:

In blissful ignorance I commenced to build myself a house. It did not even occur to me that I knew nothing about it — and what a good thing it did not; and how fortunate I was in my parents. My father was a most practical man, but he did not remark that I was embarking on something about which one needs a little experience, to say the least; neither did he remind me that I had no money.

In the end the cottage cost much less than a conventional house. With the assistance of a few friends, a devoted and hardworking nephew and a horse called Adam, the cottage was completed and made ready for occupation. Adam was indispensable. Harnessed to a rough sledge, he could haul the large packing cases from Mooroolbark station to the construction site.

Surprisingly, it was Edna's mother rather than her father who displayed the major interest and exerted most influence on the building of the cottage. Mrs Walling would

The interior of the cottage, with its bush-crafted stool and tables, had a homely, rustic quality that characterised the later buildings in Bickleigh Vale village

spend days watching the work, sitting on a box, talking over the placing of windows and fireplace — their proportions and other details. Edna wrote later:

I always felt safe if she (mother) approved for I liked her ideas. Father never came up, he didn't like the country, and was past the age when stretching his legs on a country road might have taken him there as it had in England, and so the practical problems that confronted me were discussed within the enclosure of their flat which had all the amenities and refinements I had no desire to possess. Wherever I got the strange and irresistible longing for a little pleasant cottage with nothing beyond the barest necessities of life, it certainly was not from either of my parents.

While the cottage was being built 'trees were being planted and the grounds, rather spasmodically landscaped, had at last an appearance of completion and restfulness which had been my ambition for so long'. The cottage was called 'Sonning'. As she noted herself, it was

not, perhaps a very appropriate name to have chosen for this little home in the Australian countryside, but it was inevitable. At the age of seven I was rowed on the river Thames from Reading up — or is it down — to the little hamlet of Sonning, and was so enthralled that I made a vow that when I owned my own little cottage I would call it Sonning; so deeply did the soft-sounding name become engraved on my mind that when the land became mine there was no question as to its title. Had it been in Alaska or the Sahara it would still have been Sonning.

Even when quite new, the cottage seemed to snuggle into the ground

By 1925, at the age of twenty-eight, Edna Walling was beginning to make a name for herself, despite her rather unconventional lifestyle. Sonning was relatively isolated and had none of the services offered by nearer city living. The cottage comprised a kitchen and one other room that served as office, bedroom and sitting-room. Its owner was seldom out of jodhpurs, and generally wore a broad-brimmed hat. She became a familiar sight in Mooroolbark as she motored to and fro in 'Psychi', a Fiat 509 given by her father. A car was essential for her work — to take her to country and city jobs alike, and to gather plants from various nurseries. Dressed in shirt, tie, jacket and jodhpurs, she was a regular visitor to 'Coombe Cottage', Coldstream, where she worked on the garden for Dame Nellie Melba. The famous soprano's elegantly coutured figure and chauffeured limousine must have struck an incongruous note when she paid her return visits to Sonning. But the two got on famously, even though Melba was slow to pay her fees. The design Walling produced for part of the garden was never carried out, but she was responsible for employing, supervising and paying three girl gardeners at Coombe Cottage. Melba thought nothing of departing the country for six months and leaving Edna to pay the wages. Reimbursement came in time, however, and no doubt Edna's association with the grand old lady helped to bolster her reputation. In some unpublished notes Walling describes Melba's funeral:

On our way to the cemetery our little Austin 7 was in the middle of a very long stream of cars and just as we were coming into Lilydale we ran out of petrol! What a blessing that incline was, and an even greater one was that R.A.C.V. service car on the side of the road. We rolled to a stop beside him and were very soon mobile again, and slipped in between two surprised-looking chauffeurs driving limousines!

Edna Walling as she appeared in the Australian Woman's Mirror *in 1925*

At the start of a trip to Sydney in the early 1930s, Edna (on the running-board) and her mother

These were busy days as more and more commissions were received. The garden around Sonning flourished in the rich soil and in no time foxgloves, hollyhocks and thyme were colonising the surroundings. A glade of liquidambars was planted and silver birches, which were to become an Edna Walling trademark, were established. Life was busy, simple, rustic, hard but happy.

At some time in the early 1920s an 18 acre allotment adjacent to Sonning came up for sale. As Walling later described the situation, 'my heart sagged with thoughts of poultry farms, and, even worse, weekend shacks and noisy occupants. I could not afford to own it [permanently, she meant], but I could control its destiny, and so it was decided that if built upon it must be, I would do the building'.

Borrowing heavily, Edna managed to acquire the 18 acres at £50 per acre. Surveyors were called in to subdivide the land. It was not a normal subdivision, of course, but one carefully devised by the landowner. It was indeed one of the most remarkable 'adventures in rural development' (Edna's term) that Victoria has seen. Bickleigh Vale Road (named after that Devonshire village) was established, and allotments of 1 or 2 acres drawn up.

Without any costly or complicated legal arrangements, Walling was able to control the development of the village. Prospective owners had first to be approved by their vendor, and then agree to a cottage and garden design of the vendor's making.

The new landowner deplored the 'stereotyped and unimaginative creations' which most people lived in. She saw an opportunity to demonstrate that it was possible, both economically and practically, to build cottages for people other than herself that would 'rest upon the landscape in sweet and quiet accord instead of being a dull bruise that never departs'. In her opinion, 'fitting the cottage on the landscape harmoniously, as well as to the requirements of the inmates, should direct the planning'.

The cost to the client was £100 per acre. In addition to the land, and plans for the cottage and garden, Edna provided plants and advice, and a guarantee that she would interfere in the development of the allotment! She also directed the building and garden operations, regretting the fact that she was too busy to undertake the actual labour herself. The allotments were separated by simple farm fences, broken now and then by picket gates for access to neighbours' properties. The building materials were basically the same as those of Sonning — rock, timber and wooden shingles. Early photographs of some of the cottages show that they sat in a more open landscape than they do in the 1990s. Grass ran up to the walls of the cottages, where now large trees overshadow and perennials and shrubs crowd around their bases. This is clearly how Edna saw it when she began. It was a remarkable vision — to transform an almost bare paddock into a picturesque English village. Edna threw herself enthusiastically into the project. 'I can imagine few things more satisfying and exciting than the steering of a little country village into a course that will

Raw and early days at Sonning I

Edna Walling's first plan for the subdivision of Bickleigh Vale village was published in Home Beautiful *in November 1930*

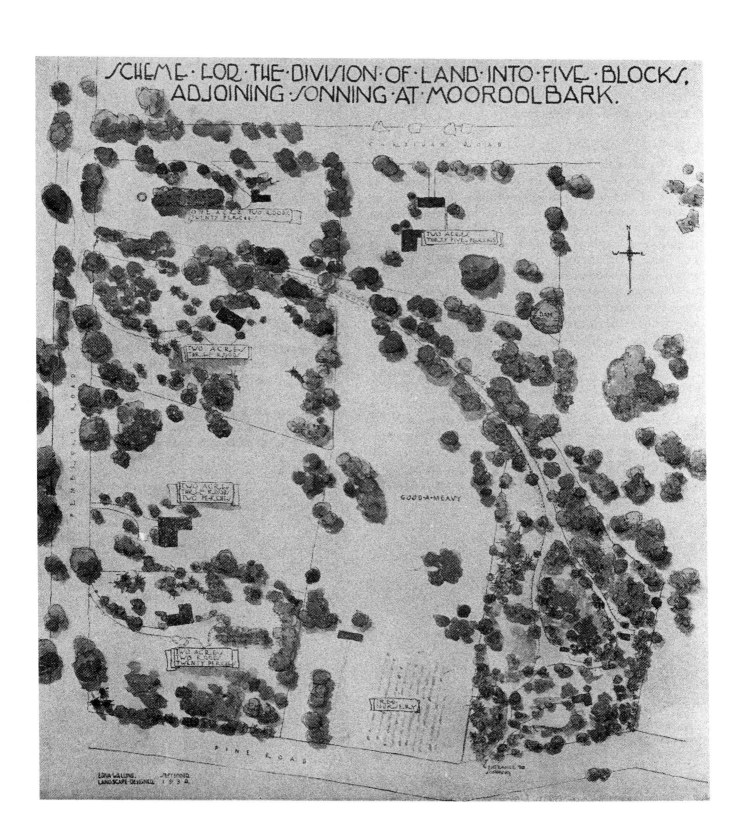

SCHEME·FOR·THE·DIVISION·OF·LAND·INTO·FIVE·BLOCKS,
ADJOINING·SONNING·AT·MOOROOLBARK.

CHRISTIAN·ROAD

N

ONE·ACRE·TWO·ROOD·
THIRTY·PERCH·

TWO·ACRES·
THIRTY·FIVE·PERCHS·

DAM

TWO·ACRES·
THREE·ROOD·

PEMBROKE·ROAD

TWO·ACRES·
ONE·ROOD·
TWO·PERCH·

GOOD·A·MEAVY

TWO·ACRES·
TWO·ROOD·
TWENTY·PERCH·

NURSERY

ENTRANCE·TO·SONNING

PINE·ROAD

EDNA·WALLING,   SEPTEMBER
LANDSCAPE·DESIGNER.   1934.

bring it to a picturesque completion when every cottage is erected, and every tree planted', she wrote in the *Australian Home Beautiful* ten years after the commencement of Bickleigh Vale village. Not until the concept of cluster housing came into its own in the early and middle 1970s did anything else of this type develop in Victoria. The 1920s subdivisions of Heidelberg and Mornington by Walter Burley Griffin are suburban and almost ordinary by comparison.

The cottages were built over a number of years and totalled sixteen in all. By 1934 the following had been constructed: 'Mistover', 'Hurst', 'Downderry', 'Good-a-Meavy' ('The Barn'), 'Lynton Lee', and an unnamed cottage on the corner of Pembroke Road and Pine Road. Sonning and its little outbuilding 'The Cabin' completed the village. There was a cheery neighbourly atmosphere among the residents, but there was never the co-operative spirit that developed in such places as 'Montsalvat', the artists' colony in Eltham, Victoria. There was no euphoria attached to the place, yet the spirit of its creator pervaded every corner of the village.

It is easy to romanticise life in the growing village in those days. There is no doubt that it was pleasant. A variety of people chose to live there: an East Melbourne newsagent used Mistover as a weekend cottage, and a teacher did the same with Lynton Lee. Others, including a solicitor and a retired couple, came to live there permanently.

What all these people had in common, though, was a knowledge and love of gardening, and an enjoyment of the simple pleasures of life. The brief provided for Lynton Lee by Edna's friend Lorna Fielden requested simply 'some lavender bushes on which to dry my handkerchiefs'. The cottages themselves were the very essence of simplicity. Door catches, hinges, gates, fireplaces and windows were as simple in detail as was the basic accommodation provided in the cottages. Walling's comment on gates in *Cottage and Garden* applies to her concept of building, both in general

Blanche Sharpe and Edna in the grounds of Sonning, at work on The Cabin

and in detail: 'The very simplest construction is always the best. As in so many other things it is better to stick to simplicity in order to escape that "novel" effect that so soon palls and stamps a thing as ordinary.'

As for the gardens of the cottages, they were guided by an expert hand, but allowed to grow and develop in the way a cottage garden should. As Edna also wrote in *Cottage and Garden*, plants were to be of

all kinds jumbled up together, the tall sheltering the low, and the fragrant justifying their presence even when their colour and form may not; a veritable patchwork of colour, a Lil-iputian [sic] fairyland of spires. Always there is a little pathway of stone or bricks, always there is lavender, and herbs and rosemary and climbing roses whenever support can be found for them.

The village continued to grow and develop into the 1940s, though in the winter of 1936 a tragic fire burnt the 15-year-old Sonning to the ground. Everything was lost — precious drawings, accounts, hundreds of priceless photographs, a

The Cabin completed: a small but charming 'adventure in amateur building'

valuable collection of pewter, and many hundreds of books, including autographed copies of Gertrude Jekyll's works and of Nellie Melba's *Melodies and Memories*. (Fourteen pairs of riding breeches, Edna's standard outfit, were also lost!) All these irreplaceable treasures, collected over forty years, were gone in a matter of minutes.

'The Cabin' became home. This tiny one-room stone cottage had been built in the garden of Sonning about 1927 and served as summer-house, studio and guest room. It measured only 15 feet by 13 feet and its construction was described by Walling in an article in the *Australian Home Beautiful* in 1928 under the heading 'How We Put Up Our Little Stone Cabin — Another Adventure in Amateur Building'. The article begins:

Some people say, when they see the cabin for the first time 'Why did you build it so far away from the house?' And the answer is, 'That's why we built it!' The height of the walls is then queried, and the answer is 'We did not build them higher than six feet because we like them six feet high!' And you can just imagine the tones of almost resentful surprise that these people adopt when they announce, 'Ten casement windows in a room so small!' But the blow extraordinary (for them) comes when they enquire, 'How are you going to finish the inside of the walls?' And we, or I, according to whether I am alone and unchampioned or supported by a trusty band of friends, reply, 'We have!'

Plans were soon drawn up for a new cottage and before long 'Sonning II' was under way. It comprised an office, sitting-room, kitchen, bathroom and attic bedroom. A further attic bedroom was added several years later. The building flowed into the landscape by incorporating piazzas, pergolas, rock paving and low walls extending into the garden.

The late 1920s, the 1930s and the 1940s were busy decades. There were cottages to be built, articles and books to be written, public lectures, open days at Sonning, camping trips to the country. As if this were not enough, Edna started her own nursery on 1½ acres adjacent to Sonning. And of course there were several hundred gardens to be designed and built, many in distant towns and on remote country properties. And the landscape designer still did not balk at getting her hands dirty when there was a special wall to be built or a delicate planting arrangement to be executed.

Throughout her life Edna Walling was able to attract people to her cause, people

At Sonning, the kitchen door looked out on the nursery

Lynton Lee — 'the building flowed into the landscape…'

who would devote themselves to her despite her sometimes difficult moods. A former employee who worked with her in the 1930s has described her as 'selfish and ruthless, but utterly delightful'. And a friend once described her as 'a definite character; but every inch a lady'.

Her employees were required to work with the same strength and devotion as their boss. And assistance she certainly needed. Fortunately for Walling she had an uncanny knack of recognising latent talent in people and utilising it to the full. Eric Hammond developed his business into a firm of outstanding landscape contractors largely because of the work she channelled through him.

Edna was also responsible for 'discovering' Ellis Stones. In the mid-1930s Ellis Stones was working as a building contractor on a house in Hawdon Street, Ivanhoe, while Edna was laying out the garden of an adjoining house. At a chance meeting she complained to Stones that she could find no one to build a decent dry-stone wall. Ellis offered to do the work, was sceptically allowed to, and more than satisfied his new friend. It was an historic meeting — 'the stuff of legends', as described by Ellis Stones's friend David Yencken, then chairman of the Australian Heritage Commission. Edna recognised Stones's talent with rockwork, whether building a wall or placing an outcrop, and encouraged and supported him. Many of the rock outcrops, walls and ponds in her gardens were, from then on, constructed by Ellis Stones. But they were two of a kind, both stubborn and strong-willed, and their relationship, although fruitful and mutually convenient, was a turbulent one. Despite all their years of bickering, however, Ellis Stones dedicated his book *Australian Garden Design* (1971) to 'Edna Walling who started me on my career'. In the same year, in a letter to 'Miss Walling' (as he called her), 'Andy' (as she called him) said that 'When I was asked to write a book on my approach to landscaping, I naturally thought of you, as we know you suggested I might do better landscaping than building'. Ellis Stones played a part in building Sonning II and other cottages and gardens in the Bickleigh Vale village, as did Eric Hammond.

Glen Wilson was another who had the benefit of her knowledge, guidance and wisdom in his early years of landscape work in the mid-1950s. He visited Edna at 'The Barn', where she was then living, once a week for lessons, paying a small fee. He recalls that at this time Edna was not busy on many commissions. After a year the designer was confident enough of her young student to allow him to take charge

The kitchen at Sonning

of some of her work. By that time she was no longer preparing the beautifully coloured landscape plans she had done in the past; a rough 6B pencil sketch on brown paper served the purpose. And, needing a contractor who would plant the gardens as she required, she gave Glen Wilson the job.

But way back in the middle 1920s, what was required was someone who could sort out the financial side of Edna's business. Money never really concerned her. She was shrewd when she wanted to be, but the day-to-day accounting in a busy practice left her cold. And so a young pharmacy graduate, Blanche Sharpe, came to Sonning about 1926. She gave up, for the time being, the possibility of a lucrative career to live at Sonning. Fifty years later she still recalls the 'appalling state of the books'. Accounts were sometimes not rendered and, if they were, there was no system to ensure that payment had been received.

There were other helpers. Alice Houghton, a neighbour, was employed in those early days to help with odd jobs. And, for 1s 6d a day, Edna for a time took her evening meals with the Houghton family.

Gwynnyth Crouch began work at Sonning in 1934. She lived in what she calls a 'man's room' attached to the potting shed in the garden, and describes her position at the time as gardener, girl Friday, 'mother', secretary, cook and clothes-mender. The days were long and the work physically exhausting. A typical day began at perhaps 6 a.m. Breakfast was prepared and the boss's clothes laid out on her bed. Plans were drawn, garden and animals attended to, nursery work undertaken, meals prepared and correspondence dealt with. On days before a town garden was to be planted they worked till midnight, lifting and balling plants in the nursery. The next day a 5 a.m. start ensured that other nurseries, usually Sparkes and McAlpine in Box Hill, could be visited on the way to town, with time left to finish the planting: a tough life considering that most planting was done in winter.

Other gardens required regular maintenance. For the first year after its completion Gwynnyth Crouch spent one day a fortnight maintaining the garden at 'Silver Birches' in Yarrbat Avenue, Balwyn, for its owner, Mr Douglas George of Melbourne's famous Georges store.

In 1926 Edna Walling began to write regularly for the *Australian Home Beautiful*, her monthly letters and articles helping to popularise her name. Often she would include garden designs for subscribers who submitted house plans to the magazine. These articles, which appeared regularly until 1934, and irregularly for some years after that, are laced with her own plans, sketches and photographs. In November 1930 the magazine published an especially fascinating plan showing the subdivision and planning of Bickleigh Vale village.

She worked with many architects, perhaps the most fashionable being Marcus Martin. Together they designed a wonderful house and formal garden for Dr Ringland Anderson in Linlithgow Avenue, Toorak. Sadly, like many of these large inner suburban gardens, it has since been subdivided. As the name of Walling became known in the wealthier quarters of Melbourne, clients began to include people like Mrs Keith Murdoch (now Dame Elisabeth), Mrs Harold Darling, Sir George Tallis, Sir Clive and Lady Steele, and Sir William and Lady Irvine. The Baillieu, Grimwade and Cato families also consulted Edna Walling on various projects. She undertook jobs at Toorak College and the Methodist Ladies College. Many of her clients lived in the city's rich middle-belt suburbs. Gardens several acres in size were then quite common and allowed considerable scope to a talented garden designer, although their owners, Edna's clients, often thought of her as a mere labourer, much to her annoyance. She refused to use a tradesman's entrance and on many occasions simply walked off the job after an altercation with a snooty client.

Apart from these large city gardens there

Dr Ringland Anderson's garden in Toorak was one of Walling's most formal gardens

Edna Walling considered that wrought iron gave 'an opportunity of expressing design with a lightness not easily obtained with other material'. This garden was designed for the Beattie family

was also work in some of the extensive hill stations of the Dandenong Ranges to the east of Melbourne and in the Macedon Ranges to the north. These provided an ideal climate for the English plants Edna favoured up until the 1950s, and their steep slopes gave her every opportunity to introduce the architectural design elements she used so well. Some of Edna Walling's best work remains in these areas, including 'Mawarra' at Sherbrooke, 'Folly Farm' at Olinda and 'Durrol' and 'Greystones' at Mount Macedon.

Country clients included the owners of some of the larger homesteads in the Western District of Victoria and the Riverina in New South Wales. Among these garden commissions were 'Boortkoi' for Mr Andrew Manifold at Hexham; 'Ardgarten' for the Youngmans at Grassdale; and 'Eurambeen' for Mrs Theo Beggs at Beaufort. Other gardens were designed for 'Warrock', 'Willaroo', 'Seven Creeks', 'Delatite', 'Naringal', 'Yalla-y-poora' and 'Allanvale'. In New South Wales there were 'Markdale', 'Willamolong' and 'Kildrummie'. There were, in fact, commissions from every state: some were built in part only and some not at all.

For preparatory work on these properties Edna, generally accompanied by one of her friends, would visit the site to take notes and any necessary measurements. She then returned to Melbourne and drew up a sketch plan, which was sent to the clients. If they wished to proceed rough estimates were prepared and a contract awarded — generally to E. H. Hammond. She would then visit the site with Hammond and his team and assist in setting out the design on the ground. From then on it was left to the contractor. Often on final inspection Walling would insist on changes, and they were not always simple changes. A whole wall or flight of stairs might have to be shifted to give a better vista or a more pleasing proportion. For the city gardens she liked to be approached at an early stage in the house design. This gave her the opportunity to comment on the siting and design of the house. She considered herself, justifiably, as something of an expert on this matter. But her early involvement was all too rare.

As we have seen, she was not daunted by the rich and fashionable people she worked for, and became particularly irritated when some of the wealthy clients objected to her fee — rarely more than £20 to £30 for the largest garden. A surviving account from a garden designed for Mr A. M. Wann of 'Sunningdale', Benalla, Victoria, and dated 1 December 1936, gives some indication of her charges.

The terrace and pergola at Eurambeen in Victoria's western district

May 7th	To advisory visit	£ 2	2	0
July 9th	To Garden Plan and Plant Lists	6	6	0
August 26	To visit in connection with super-			
	vision of construction and planting	3	13	6
September 14	To Planting Visit	2	2	0
November 24	To Planting Visit	2	2	0
	To Travelling Expenses (four visits)	5	7	0
		£21	12	6

It is worth noting that the cost of the plants for the same job was £34 5s 8d. A year later, following one more visit, a further account was rendered, consisting of £4 3s 0d for professional fees and £11 18s 6d for additional plants.

Walling had a reputation for being expensive, but there seems little foundation for this as far as her own fee was concerned. The construction of the garden, however, was another matter. This often included major structural work such as rock walls, stairs, pergolas, ponds and rock outcrops. The cost of such work could amount to several hundred pounds.

As has been indicated, these large gardens were most often constructed by Eric Hammond. Edna's long and happy association with Hammond commenced in about 1926. He was one of the few men she respected and admired, insisting on calling him Mr Hammond, while he always called her Edna, for her entire life. Despite her sometimes outrageous demands that completed works be dramatically altered, Eric Hammond now recalls that they 'never had an argument'. In the 1920s he was largely engaged on building cottages at the village. A quote for one of these states simply, 'To cottage similar to Mrs Walling's, with 10' x 12' bedroom added — £311.0.0d'. But these were the days when a quote meant a fixed price, and within that figure there was considerable latitude. Details were worked out as they went along, and often Walling would lend a hand at rock-walling or chimney-making. It was essential that their relationship was not too businesslike, since it needed to allow scope for the designer to change her mind. For instance she noticed one day that the rough side of fibrous plaster had much more character and appeal than the smooth side, and insisted that all the sheets be put on back to front.

In a letter to Hammond in 1959 Edna showed awareness of a potential danger in their long collaboration:

I feel sure that you will not misunderstand me when I ask you not to give too much away in your association with other landscape designers.

Having been practically the sole contractor of my jobs during almost a lifetime of work, you have been in a unique position and I would not like our happy association to be marred by any feeling of resentment on my part for the sake of a mere word of appeal.

As you know, any designing ability I may have is not the result of any university course or any other tuition but is purely a gift from above and, apart from being my bread and butter, I am eternally grateful for it and feel that I must guard it against any duplication.

It must always be remembered that ideas are one thing and their right application is another. You will I know realise that discrimination in the matter of the recipients of these ideas and experiences is rather important to me.

Edna Walling in the 1940s

The reference to 'a gift from above' suggests that Edna held religious beliefs: she was in fact a devout Christian Scientist.

Even as a child, and all through her life, Edna had had a passion for building. At times she could be irritable and moody, and never more so than when she was not actively engaged on some building project or other. By the end of the 1940s building at Bickleigh Vale village had come to an end. But another village was forming in Edna Walling's mind. She had often travelled along the Great Ocean Road to Lorne, where the scenery, with giant blue gums marching down to the water's edge, had special appeal. Her acquisition, in 1948, of a 16 acre block wooded with ironbarks and blue gums on steeply sloping land at East Point, 7 miles east of Lorne, set her fertile mind on the trail of a village by the seaside. In characteristic style she first set about building herself a cottage. With the aid of a few friends and some local tradesmen it was 'hitched on to the side of this one-in-three hillside with our own fair hands!' Brandishing a trowel, Walling accomplished most of the rockwork herself. And there was plenty of that, including a 'built-in' stone staircase and a room underneath with a rock wall incorporating various seats and shelves. The track into the cottage was surveyed in typically irregular manner with 'the offsider walking ahead with a handkerchief tied to the end of a broomstick so that I could see her wending her way through the trees, calling to her to keep up a little or down a little until we eventually struck the road'.

East Point was one of Edna's favourite places. Late in life she wrote an unpublished manuscript about it called 'The Happiest Days of My Life'. She used the cottage and its surrounding bushland as a retreat in which to rest and gather inspiration. So enchanted was she with the new holiday cottage that Walling could not bring herself to develop her idea of a village by the sea. Instead she enjoyed the peace and seclusion of this isolated spot. Unfortunately in the late 1950s this cottage too was destroyed by fire, and on Edna's departure from Victoria in 1967 she gave the property to the Bird Observers' Club, which uses it frequently.

Even in her last few years she longed to build. At Buderim in Queensland, where she moved in 1967, she set her sights on developing an Italian-style village that would tumble down the hillside of a natural amphitheatre. She chose a beautiful site, but her age (she was then in her seventies) prevented her from proceeding.

A corner of the garden in the village Edna laid out at Mt Kembla, NSW

She tried valiantly but unsuccessfully to interest a Melbourne-based developer in the idea, but that village never proceeded beyond a few hasty sketches.

Two other villages were designed. One in New South Wales was built, and the other at Port Pirie in South Australia only reached the report stage. Fortunately the plans for both survive. The client in both cases was Broken Hill Associated Smelters Pty Ltd. In the late 1940s Edna was invited to meet the general manager, who asked her to help with the siting of several houses for their coalmine at Mount Kembla in New South Wales. The design required four houses to be placed on a hillside backed by dense rainforest with a view over Lake Illawarra. Within hours of arriving at Mount Kembla Edna had abandoned the house plans she had been given, had won over the mine manager, and was directing a front-end loader to shift giant boulders around the house sites she had chosen: 'I soon realised that here was an opportunity not to be missed. It was such a treat to have men and machinery so geared to carry out one's ideas instead of a whole gang of men standing limply around waiting for a slow-witted boss to make use of them.' (She was rarely complimentary about men!) Returning to Melbourne she had the general manager employ a young female architect to redesign the houses. Together they pushed around small models of the houses on a contour plan until a satisfactory result was achieved. Passing through that country some years later Edna found 'it was most gratifying to see how pleasantly the little gardens were nestled up to the huge boulders we had placed, and how well those houses looked'.

Throughout these years Edna Walling was writing: for the *Australian Home Beautiful* and other magazines, for newspapers, and for Oxford University Press, which published her four books. Like the articles, the books helped her to gain popularity and made her ideas widely known. By 1950 over 11 400 copies of her three books on gardens had been sold.

The first book, *Gardens in Australia — Their Design and Care*, was published in 1943. It was a sellout, and a second edition was printed the following year. By 1950 it had gone into four editions. It is an utterly charming, yet most practical book. Its author drew on her wealth of experience in designing gardens for more than twenty years, and used her own photographs and sketches to illustrate her points. Here one can find out the ideal proportions for garden steps; how to make a pergola; how to grow a thyme lawn; hints on building low stone walls; using sculpture in the garden; and so on. The thirty-two brief sections have such diverse headings as The lesson of the natural country; Water in the country garden; The gentle art of pruning; Picture making with trees and shrubs; Back doorways; and Landscaping the window box.

Throughout these disparate chapters Edna, in her delightfully intimate and easy prose, wins over the reader to her philosophy of garden design. She sums this up in the foreword:

Who shall say this tree must be so far from its fellows, and that shrub so remote from its neighbours, for is not the joyous garden the one in which the happy association of plants is largely accidental? The garden laid out with all the scientific skill of the trained horticulturist so often misses that divine something found in gardens planted with the affectionate hands of those who personally tend their plants.

The second book, *Cottage and Garden in Australia*, followed four years later, in 1947:

Here then is a book of cottages — quite commonplace cottages, but they do, perhaps, just escape the stereotyped and unimaginative creations of which one grows so weary, and they may prove a liniment to some who begin to think how hopeless it is to achieve the cottage they rapturously long for.

The cottages were those of Edna's own subdivision, of course, and the book provides a guide to everything from the plans, specifications and detailed drawings to hints on choosing the cottage china. Kenneth Grahame's description of Badger's kitchen in *The Wind in the Willows* is quoted as inspiration for the cottage owner. Part of the book's value lies in its inclusion of over one hundred excellent photographs of cottages at Bickleigh Vale village, many of which are now altered almost beyond recognition. There are more than thirty-five photographs and sketches and a good description of Sonning II, which now retains only one room (the tiny office) that resembles its original condition.

A Gardener's Log, which appeared in 1948, is a collection of some of Edna Walling's articles from the *Australian Home Beautiful*. In his introduction to the second edition (1969), the Director of the Royal Botanic Gardens in Melbourne, R. T. M. Pescott, said:

while not containing anything immediately new, [*A Gardener's Log*] will serve to inform the new gardener, and remind the older gardener, that in their midst is a landscape designer who has created a new concept of horticulture which could reasonably become the basis for a universally accepted style of Australian landscaping. In *A Gardener's Log* she sets out to record the day to day observations of what she has done, quoting both failures and successes, but making the reader feel that he is receiving a personally escorted tour of something that is very precious to the designer and creator.

By the 1950s Walling was becoming more and more preoccupied with conservation problems. Her fourth book, *The Australian Roadside* (published in 1952), reflects this concern. In the preface to the book she says:

To say so much in an appeal for the observation and conservation of the natural roadside beauty was not my original intention, but the continual scenes of unthinking devastation have made it difficult to remain quiet, and it is hoped that in consequence of this book, some readers may not continue to view the roadside plants as so much 'scrub' but as the very interesting, fitting and invaluable plants they really are.

This book not only indicates Edna Walling's great love of the Australian countryside but also demonstrates her detailed knowledge of the Australian flora. Perhaps the most remarkable feature of this book, though, is the short, prophetic chapter on 'Roadside Ecology'. She argues strongly and lucidly for an ecological approach to highway landscaping.

So vital to the future of the countryside is a keen understanding of native plants *as they appear on the landscape* that the ecological approach is the only approach to roadside planting. To know what species will survive under any particular conditions is not enough. For instance, in Australia, as incongruous on the Victorian highway as any exotics can be the planting of Western Australian gums or plants from a Queensland rain forest; the Victorian scene is distinct, and the Queensland scene is distinct; and it is vital that we should preserve the individuality not only of each State, but also of each district in that State. We must therefore look about for the best way to do any roadside planting so that it will not interfere with, but will emphasise, the natural character of the country through which the highway passes.

These were not completely new ideas to Edna Walling in the 1950s. As early as September 1937 she had had an article published in the *Argus* entitled 'Roadside Planting — Fitting the Highway into the Landscape'. Half a century later conservationists are still fighting the same battle. *Eucalyptus forrestiana*, *Melaleuca armillaris* and *Acacia baileyana* continue to be planted in vast quantities along Victorian roadsides from Mildura to Mallacoota.

It was over twenty years after the appearance of *The Australian Roadside* that a forum on roadside conservation resulted in the publication of the forum papers and the establishment of the Roadside Conservation Committee. But Walling's book

The busy road just outside Little Milton's long, narrow front garden seems a world away, so skilfully is it screened

still remains the basic text on the Victorian roadside. As she notes at the end of the book, 'The roadside is the Front Garden of the Nation'. Later she wrote a sequel to the book and called it 'The Front Garden of the Nation'. It was largely a collection of her photographs of roads and roadside vegetation, but no publisher could be found for it.

She wrote another book, *On the Trail of Australian Wildflowers*, in the late 1940s but it too failed to find a publisher. It was not until 1984, eleven years after her death, that it emerged from Mulini Press. This book reinforces her deep attachment to the Australian landscape, her knowledge and pleasure of its rich variety and her formidable command of its plants and its ecology.

The 1950s saw a change in the direction of Edna Walling's efforts. Tighter economic conditions and increased labour costs made the construction of large private gardens almost prohibitive. In any case, by the middle of the century Walling was fifty-four

The Barn, Edna's last home in Victoria. The breezeway appears, at this stage, to be partly enclosed

years old and had already achieved more than many other people would have contemplated in a lifetime.

During this period Edna made two other quite remarkable changes. She left her beloved Sonning. And she almost totally rejected the use of exotic plants in favour of native species.

She left Sonning for several reasons. It had become too large for her to cope with alone, and it was impossible to find a suitable assistant. But perhaps more importantly, she had become, through her writings, inseparably linked with that cottage and its garden. The 'No admittance' sign on the gate did little to deter members of her admiring public, who arrived in a steady stream. She discovered that it was not glamorous to be famous. In 1929 she had written of having 'sketched for a neighbour a little plan for a stable, garage, feed and harness room, with workshop and man's room above. Into this sketch was embodied her especial desire to have an opening right through the centre of the building to a courtyard beyond'. Now in the early 1950s she planned to convert 'The Barn' (otherwise known as 'Good-a-Meavy') to a house for her own use. With characteristic energy she toiled away, building a brick chimney with her own hands. It was far from being a conventional house. The open breezeway was retained (although closed in at a later date), making for a chilly journey from kitchen to sitting-room. The Barn had been constructed in 1929 using 'five motor packing cases at 50/- each, five to six loads of stone, costing 5/- a load, timber for the framework amounting to £15, and the galvanised iron for the roof, approximately £12'.

Her change to the almost exclusive use of natives was remarkable. Eric Hammond recalls that it happened 'almost overnight'. This is not to suggest that up until then she had only used exotic plants. Quite the contrary. Edna Walling was one of the first to recognise the unique aesthetic qualities of Australia's indigenous plants, together with the practical common sense of using them in garden designs. As early as the mid-1920s she had extolled the virtues of many of our native plants in her magazine articles. They were not the dominant species she used in her gardens by any means, but at least they were part of her palette. In one of these early articles, later reprinted in *A Gardener's Log*, she states:

I am not a fanatic where native plants are concerned; I could not manage without many plants that come from other lands (Westmore Thyme for instance!) and much as I believe that in certain places we should studiously exclude the exotics and strive to recreate the natural scene — not a simple task — I think it is neither necessary nor desirable to consider where a plant comes from for the average home garden, so long as we enjoy it just for itself and so long as it harmonises with its neighbour's foliage and flowers.

The silver birch had been one of her favourite trees from the moment she began to design gardens, and she was probably more responsible than any other person for popularising its use in domestic gardens in Victoria. She loved to scatter birches about in natural clumps, contrasting their white paper-like trunks with a background of dark green foliage. It is hard to believe that the same person in the middle 1950s, in response to a comment that the white trunks of birch trees gave a similar effect to some of the white-trunked eucalypts, should reply 'Then why use the birches!'

Friends and colleagues from these times have suggested that for a number of years Walling had become more aware of and more interested in native plants. This is certainly borne out in *The Australian Roadside*, which was published, as we have seen, in 1952. It would appear that in some short space of time the notion of a purely native garden crystallised in her mind to such an extent that she could see no reason why anyone should persist with exotic plants in the Australian environment.

By the 1950s Ellis Stones likewise was campaigning for a more general acceptance of the use of native plant species. Whether Stones's association with Edna influenced her is not known, but it was most likely one of a number of factors. Others at the time were also becoming interested in native plants. Dulcie and Ben Schubert were two of the leaders in Victoria's natives movement. (It was while working at the Schuberts' nursery about 1955 or 1956 that Glen Wilson met Edna Walling. As he says in the introduction to his book, 'Through the Schuberts' connection with the late Miss Edna Walling, I had the good fortune to enjoy a period of study with that great lady' [*Landscaping with Australian Plants*, 1975].)

Other native plants enthusiasts were Jean Galbraith, the botanist and author, who assisted Edna for many years with plant identification and wrote detailed captions for many of the photographs in her unpublished manuscripts; and Thistle Harris, who had been active in this field since the 1920s, as Edna knew. And Miss Harris says that soon after the first edition of her *Wildflowers of Australia* was published in 1938, Edna drove from Melbourne to Sydney in one day to see her.

This multi-trunk silver birch in the Marshall garden would have received Edna's approval

The technical advances achieved during World War II were beginning to make a significant impact on the Australian environment by the 1950s, and the peaceful countryside around Mooroolbark did not escape. Protests from Edna Walling appeared in newspapers from time to time. She wrote on anything from her favourite causes like roadside vegetation to rather more obscure subjects, as in a fiery letter to the *Age* in March 1949 condemning zoos as 'these disgraceful institutions in our midst'. Newspapers and magazines received a continual flow of her articles for publication. Some were accepted, but many were not. Most were concerned with various environmental issues. For instance in November 1950 she submitted an article to the *Herald* in which she presented a well-argued case for the exclusive use of indigenous planting in all the landscape work to be done for the 1956 Olympiad. She fought a long and bitter campaign in the 1960s to prevent the construction of a restaurant and car park on the top of Mount Dandenong. In a desperate but unsuccessful effort to forestall the project, she prepared an alternative plan. She was also on the scene in the early days of the Lake Pedder fiasco, and strongly favoured the cessation of sand-mining on Fraser Island.

Edna Walling in about 1967,
shortly before she moved to
Buderim in Queensland

By the end of Enda's life five more manuscripts had been prepared — largely collections of her photographs, with skimpy texts — but they all failed to find a publisher. These works were 'On the Trail of Australian Wildflowers' (published 1984), 'The Harvest of a Quiet Eye', 'The Happiest Days of My Life', 'Gardens of Australia' (a sequel to the earlier book of that name) and 'The Front Garden of the Nation'.

Photography was a passion she indulged all her life, and the photographs that appear in her books are more than simply illustrative: they convey the essence of their subjects. Edna was no conventional photographer, as her books testify. She thought nothing of pointing her camera directly into the sun, often with dramatic effect. That camera was constantly by her side when she travelled extensively through the eastern states, generally driving herself, with a friend to keep her company.

She visited Tasmania, where she delighted in the simple stone cottages. (Photographs of some of these buildings are used in *Cottage and Garden in Australia* to illustrate fine stonework.) Then there were visits to Inman Valley in South Australia where she was designing a house for Sir Edward Holden, the founder and chairman of General Motors Holden Ltd in Australia. Sir Edward had been so taken by the design of the cottages when he visited Bickleigh Vale village that he had abandoned his architect and employed Edna. But his sudden death in 1947 prevented the construction of the Inman Valley house. An invitation from Lady Gowrie, wife of the Governor-General, took Edna to Canberra to work on a section of the garden at Yarralumla. (On an unexpected return visit to Sonning Lady Gowrie, in the vice-regal Rolls Royce, found Walling up to her ears in compost in the nursery.)

Trips were made to Sydney to design a garden for Sir Frank Packer, to Crookwell in New South Wales for a Dr Broadbent, and for the Ashtons at 'Markdale' and 'Willamolong'. Later in life Edna made frequent visits to Queensland, where she designed a large garden for Mr Arnold Roberts at Buderim.

And of course she was constantly on the move throughout Victoria, with gardens to design and supervise in Horsham, Casterton, St Arnaud, Benalla, Ararat and Mansfield among many others. On trips to all these places her camera was never far from reach — ready to capture an unusual lighting effect or a rare flower.

Whether she was constructing a chimney at The Barn or poring over a difficult design problem, there were generally the strains of a Beethoven or Tchaikovsky symphony wafting across the lawns at Sonning. Edna Walling was as passionate about music as she was about building. Sonning, especially during the war years, became a regular place for concerts of all sorts. A flat grassed area at the bottom of the garden served as a stage and the nearby cabin as a dressing-room. Members of the forces on leave in Melbourne were always welcome to spend a relaxed day at Sonning, and the garden was frequently used as a venue for Red Cross fund-raising activities.

By the mid-1960s the suburbs were approaching Bickleigh Vale village. There were continual battles to save one or other of Edna's favourite landmarks. Her steady stream of newspaper articles and letters failed to prevent the electricity poles and concrete kerbs overtaking the original winding tracks cut through the bush. Gradually the little brick veneer boxes with their manicured gardens began to litter the surrounding countryside. The closer they came, and the less her advice was heeded, the more depressed Edna Walling became. For several years she had made an annual visit to Buderim in Queensland where she enjoyed the warmer climate and the proximity to her niece, Barbara Barnes. Edna had also visited the area a number of times while laying out the garden of her friend Arnold Roberts. She now decided to move permanently to Buderim. Although seventy-one, and saddened by her departure from the village nearly half a century after she had set it on its course, she looked forward to the change.

A little cottage called 'Bendles' was to become her new home. Buderim is some sixty miles north of Brisbane and the climate is ideal for gardening. She later wrote of finding Bendles:

No sooner had I set foot in it than I fell completely in love with it. That it was for sale and that my friends did not want it seemed too good to be true. That there were two huge Jacaranda trees which made a lovely shady lawn at the back, and also created a background to the cottage which every house needs, added tremendously to its value to me.

To sever her ties with the village and her friends in Melbourne must have taken great courage. But it was not long before her old friend Lorna Fielden, 'the mistress of Lynton Lee', also came to reside in Buderim. The two had quite different but complementary characters. Lorna Fielden had been largely responsible for getting Edna Walling's four books together. Indeed she had compiled and edited *A Gardener's Log,* and had written verse inspired by the cottages and gardens of Bickleigh Vale village.

*Lynton Lee might well have
inspired lyrical outbursts*

Although now feeling her age, Walling kept herself busy. Bendles was renovated and the garden landscaped. So too was that of Miss Fielden's new cottage. A small trickle of commissions came in and three of her unpublished manuscripts were written. She also collected together many miscellaneous articles she had written over the years and began to organise them into a publication to be called *Braggadocio*. A compulsive writer and reader, she would sit up until the early hours of the morning jotting down her thoughts and ideas. The legacy of these years remains in piles

A corner of the Roberts's garden at Buderim — one of Edna's last commissions

of notes, many scrawled in her almost illegible handwriting on the first scrap of paper that came to hand.

Edna was delighted when *A Gardener's Log* was reprinted in 1969. And what a surprise to read in the revised foreword: 'O yes, this garden of mine is not going to be a fashionable one of native plants; much as I love natives. My garden will be stuffed full of as many of the old world flowers as I can find that will thrive happily in this rather humid climate.' She had determinedly used only native plants in the preceding twenty years, but now she returned to her earlier favourites.

But as the years passed by she became more frail and less able to work. Before she left Melbourne Edna had suffered a mild stroke. Two more followed in Queensland and with each, much to her frustration, her physical abilities were further impaired. Her housekeeper and secretary, Mavis Morris, nursed a very difficult patient as best she could, but after the last stroke Edna was moved to the Selangor Private Hospital near Buderim. She died there on the night of 8 August 1973.

Even in the last few weeks in hospital her mind was active, despite her frailty. She fumed that she was not well enough to finish all her projects or to begin new ones. But what she left behind is a legacy of ideas, both gentle and charming in their detail and simplicity, yet penetrating in their depth of vision.

CHAPTER TWO:
THE MAKING
OF A GARDEN DESIGNER

Like that of most people, Edna Walling's work was influenced by a great many factors. The outside influences were, however, a matter of the fine tuning of already well-formed ideas. Few people she knew personally affected her thinking or her work. She relied more on books and magazines, and her surviving papers are a jumble of newspaper clippings, rough notes, quotations from various sources, poems and photographs. The houses of American architect Royal Barry Wills in architectural magazines, Lewis Mumford's *The Culture of Cities* and *The Image of the City*, and books on Italian gardens were all favourites. But perhaps the books she enjoyed most were those by the English artist and plantswoman Gertrude Jekyll, published between 1899 and 1937. When Edna finished her course at Burnley Horticultural College she was an enthusiastic supporter of the principles propounded by Gertrude Jekyll, who was later frequently quoted in Edna's own writings.

Jekyll was fifty-three years older than Edna, having been born in 1843. She moved in London's intellectual and artistic circles and counted John Ruskin and William Morris among her acquaintances. She trained as an artist at the Kensington School of Art in the early 1860s. Through failing eyesight she was forced to abandon paint-

Mawarra, considered by Walling to be her best garden — one she described as 'a symphony in steps and beautiful trees'

ing, and instead turned to gardening. She became one of the leaders in the controversies of the world of English garden design in the late nineteenth and early twentieth centuries. Indeed she was still in active practice when she died in 1932 at the age of eighty-nine. During her lifetime she was associated with the design of 350 gardens, ranging in size from enormous country estates to a garden for the Queen's doll's house. Her fifteen books, especially *Wood and Garden, Home and Garden* and *Colour in the Flower Garden,* published respectively in 1899, 1900 and 1908, outline her philosophy and demonstrate her practical knowledge. Gertrude Jekyll rejected the formal designs of the nineteenth century. She was essentially an artist and was one of the first to see clearly the aesthetic value and possibilities of both the colours and the architectural forms of plants.

Apart from Jekyll, two other prominent figures had moulded the English public's gardening taste at the end of the nineteenth century. William Robinson, who published his voluminous and outstanding *English Flower Garden* in 1883, was opposed to the prevailing taste of geometric beds cut into lawns, of carpet bedding and of bright colours, and instead advocated an informal gardening style based on blending flowering shrubs and perennial plants, in the total absence of architectural features. Sir Reginald Bloomfield on the other hand responded to Robinson's ideas by publishing *The Formal Garden of England* (1892), in which he promoted all that Robinson despised. The two men held diametrically opposed views and waged a lengthy press campaign against each other. It was left to Gertrude Jekyll to synthesise the views of Robinson and Bloomfield, although she clearly had a preference for the former's work.

William Robinson was a fanatical advocate of 'the wild garden', writing a book with this title in 1870. To Robinson, as Derek Clifford has noted in his *History of Garden Design* (1962), 'The best kind of garden should arise out of its site as happily as a primrose out of a cool bank'. Jekyll never took this principle of natural gardening as far as Robinson. Hers was a much more romantic approach, where structural elements and formal shapes were an important part of the design. Like Robinson, she favoured the hardy varieties of flowers in a natural planting. Unlike Robinson, she was happy to allow a seemingly casual planting arrangement to be used in the rigid geometric shape of a border or garden bed. Derek Clifford described her gardens thus: 'The result was a geometric garden with a difference. The terrace for

This photograph first appeared in Gardens in Australia. *The pergola, of white plastered pillars and saplings, is festooned with* Clematis montana

example lost its balustrades and became a dry wall, hinting at a horizontal line beneath its garment of hanging and climbing plants, rather than stating it.'

The following words, introducing Gertrude Jekyll's book *Wood and Garden* in 1899, could have been written by Edna Walling:

I have lived among outdoor flowers for many years, and have not spared myself in the way of actual labour, and have come to be on closely intimate and friendly terms with a great many growing things, and have acquired certain instincts which, though not clearly defined, are of the nature of useful knowledge.

Walling likewise possessed this elusive, intuitive feeling for garden design. It is interesting to note that an early woman landscape designer in the United States of America, Beatrix Jones Farrand (1872–1959), was similarly influenced by Jekyll, and that the work of these three women remains of major influence and significance in their respective countries. Writing of Farrand's work, Professor Marlene Salon has noted three distinctive features: her interest in native plant materials, the English influence in her work, and her ecological approach to landscape design. These three characteristics were also found in Walling's landscaping. (It would appear, however, that the two women were unaware of each other's work.)

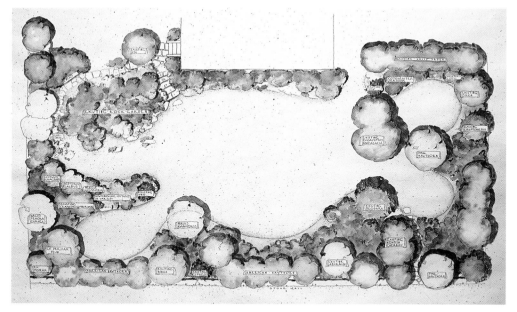

Edna's plan for Folly Farm

A view from the verandah

It is impossible not to make comparisons between Edna Walling's *A Gardener's Log* and Gertrude Jekyll's *Wood and Garden,* and it seems likely that Edna moulded her book on the latter. The Walling book is clearly adapted from short articles on a variety of topics. It nevertheless is structured similarly to Jekyll's and uses the same personal style of writing. Under four main headings corresponding to the seasons are 261 miscellaneous anecdotes. Many tell of the day-to-day activity in the Sonning garden. Others describe specific plants and still others offer practical advice on mulching, staking, scything and paving. It is a treasure trove of information and inspiration written by one who not only has an intimate knowledge and love of plants, but also a confident design ability.

Apart from the similarity between the writings of Jekyll and Walling, there are many other points of common interest. They were both concerned to achieve a harmonious relationship between house and garden. On a more personal level, they both remained spinsters, both had a love of children and animals, and they shared a passion for photography. And could it just be coincidence that they both designed gardens called 'Folly Farm', and Jekyll one called 'Bickleigh'?

There can be no doubt that Walling was greatly influenced by Jekyll. Indeed Mrs Walling, after a visit to England, brought back to her daughter signed copies of some of Jekyll's books. They held a cherished place on her bookshelves until the fire of 1936 destroyed them, along with many other highly valued possessions.

But in practical terms Jekyll's influence can be seen in many of the existing structural components of the gardens Edna designed: many pergolas, gates, walls and paths are similar to Jekyll's in both concept and detail. Walling, however, was dealing with a less affluent clientele than the fabulously rich English gentry who employed Jekyll. Nor did Australia have the skilled craftsmen available in England. Walling, therefore, was forced to interpret Jekyll's ideas in a simpler form, and it could be argued that the restraint she was compelled to use resulted in more restful gardens than those of Jekyll. Both used a strong structural layout (in Jekyll's case this was often designed by Sir Edwin Lutyens), and both then covered it with a delicate mantle of planting which softened its form and created a 'picture'.

The best-known garden designer in Victoria before Edna Walling was William Guilfoyle. He died in 1912, two years before the Walling family arrived in Australia. The Melbourne Botanic Gardens, his greatest creation, were well known to Edna and she regarded them as a landscape masterpiece. Yet she writes very little about Guilfoyle and his garden, although there is much in her work that bears comparison with his.

From Australian Home Beautiful, *an ensemble of typical Walling details: stone walls and paving, timber colonnade and semi-circular steps*

The curving lines of Folly Farm are similar to the flowing forms that Guilfoyle used so often; and the views, perspective and tantalising glimpses that interested him were all part of Edna Walling's design repertoire. For Edna, who had such a keen eye, the Royal Botanic Gardens must have provided valuable lessons. Guilfoyle's planting in the Botanic Gardens was more catholic than Edna preferred, however, and it is hard to imagine her liking Guilfoyle's architectural palm trees dotted across the lawns.

Walling dominated the garden design scene in Victoria so much from the 1920s to the 1950s that it is very easy to gain the impression that she was the only person professionally engaged in this activity at the time. This was not the case. There were other garden designers, mostly women in the early days; later they were joined by men such as John Stevens, Ellis Stones and Glen Wilson. But in the early part of Walling's career other female designers were her main competition. Milly Gibson, for instance, was a designer of some note — so much so that Walling asked her (unsuccessfully) if she would be interested in forming a partnership. The two women had been friends at Burnley, and it was no coincidence that Gibson was also a strong advocate of the work of Jekyll and Robinson.

Gibson managed a small private practice, wrote a garden page for the *Argus,* taught at Burnley, and had a vague interest in native plants. She probably deserves more credit than anyone else in Victoria for promoting large-scale industrial landscape design. Among her major landscape projects were the Shell Refinery at Geelong, the Vacuum Oil Terminal at Altona, the Glaxo factory at Bayswater, and the Maribyrnong Migrant Hostel. It is ironic that Gibson was too busy to design her own brother's garden, 'Appledore' in Eaglemont (page 81), and Edna Walling did the job instead.

In 1918 Gibson, then Milly Grassick, had taken a teaching position from Olive Holttum (later Olive Mellor) at Burnley Horticultural College. Holttum had commenced the course at Burnley in 1914 as the first full-time female student and became the first woman instructor in 1916. She remained active in the garden design world and when eventually Walling's

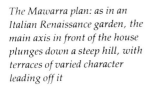

The Mawarra plan: as in an Italian Renaissance garden, the main axis in front of the house plunges down a steep hill, with terraces of varied character leading off it

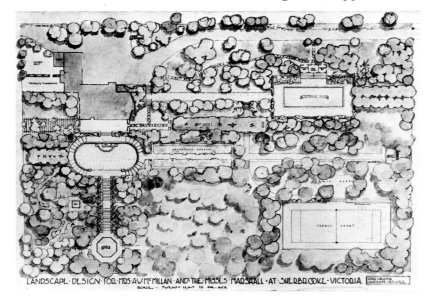

LANDSCAPE·DESIGN·FOR·MRS·A·V·McMILLAN·AND·THE·MISSES·MARSHALL·AT·SHERBROOKE·VICTORIA.

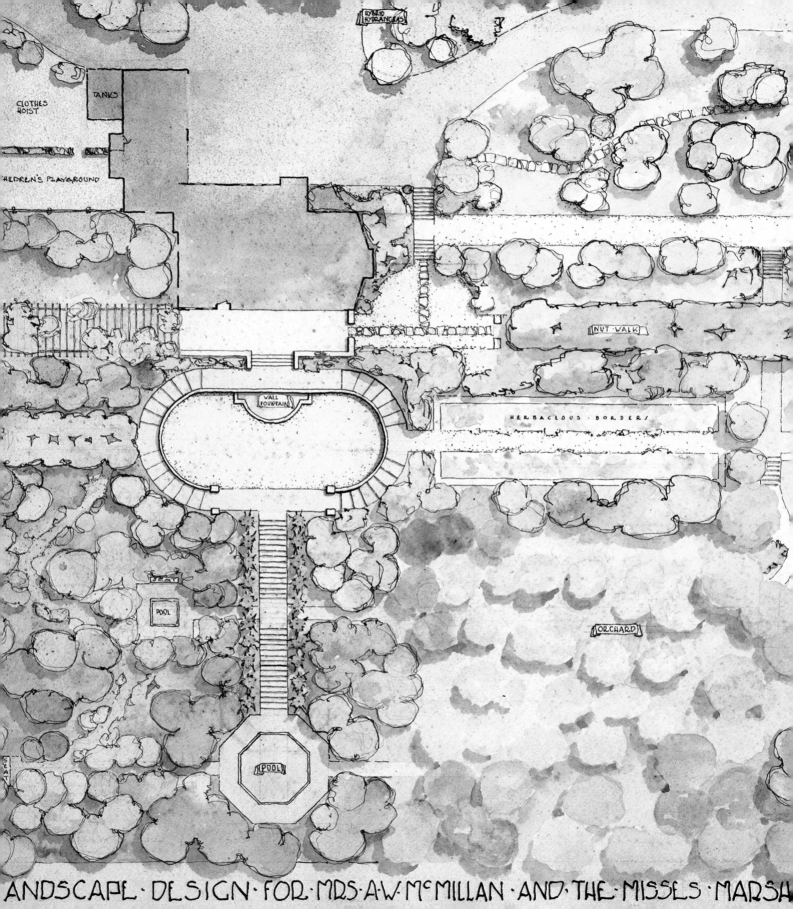

CLOTHES
HOIST

TANKS

HYBRID
HYDRANGEAS

HILDREN'S PLAYGROUND

NUT WALK

WALL
FOUNTAIN

HERBACEOUS BORDERS

SEAT

POOL

ORCHARD

SEAT

POOL

ANDSCAPE · DESIGN · FOR · MRS · A·W· McMILLAN · AND · THE · MISSES · MARSA

eccentricities became too much for the editor of the *Australian Home Beautiful* in the mid-1930s, Mellor replaced her as regular garden contributor. Olive Mellor recalled that she designed over 500 gardens during her career, even more than Edna Walling.

Joan Anderson, who was to become Joan Jones, was also a contemporary of Edna Walling, having completed the course at Burnley in the early 1920s. In 1927 she was engaged by Walling at a weekly salary of £3 15s 0d to work at Coombe Cottage for Nellie Melba. In the following year she travelled to England where she met

The fountain terrace at Mawarra is enveloped by two large stepped ramps. A huge staircase plunges down the hill from this terrace, terminating in an octagonal reflecting pool

Gertrude Jekyll, then aged eighty-five. At 'Cameron Lodge' on Mount Macedon she later designed the large pool, with its classical temple set on an island in the middle.

Among Edna Walling's favourite books were those on Italian gardens, as has been indicated. Although she had never been to Italy she had a passion for the Italian gardening style. There are certainly similarities in concept between some of the classic Italian gardens and some of the grander of Walling's. This is particularly so in the large formal gardens she designed in the 1920s and 1930s. In an article entitled 'The Italian Influence in Our Australian Gardens', published in the *Australian Home Beautiful* in 1933, she describes her 'Italian influenced' garden 'Warrawee', designed for Mrs Harold Darling in Orrong Road, Toorak. The article begins:

There is little doubt that as we advance in the designing of our gardens in Australia, we shall derive more and more inspiration from the old gardens of Italy. The chief elements of the Italian garden — stone, water and trees — are most appropriate to the conditions governing the construction of gardens in Australia.

It is interesting to note that this garden had been originally designed by the fashionable architect Walter Butler in 1910. Butler too was interested in Italian gardens and had presented a lecture to the Royal Victorian Institute of Architects in 1903 entitled 'Garden Design in Relation to Architecture'.

Italian gardens generally have a very strong and formal structure with nodal points highlighted by water, sculpture and dramatic vistas. The distinguishing feature in a Walling garden was the planting. The Italian planting is colourless and its form is used to reinforce the structure of the garden. Walling's on the other hand was soft, delicate, and subtly coloured, designed to soften the rigid architectural form.

Walling was a great admirer of the Italian practice of terracing. She recognised the importance of varying the character and design of terraces. 'Each terrace is a separate garden; one may be a parterre, one a maze of tall clipped hedges, one a lawn or paved area, and yet another a setting for water features', she noted in *A Gardener's Log*.

She also admired the smaller urban courtyard spaces of Italian cities, considering them ideal for Australian climatic conditions. The Italian-style village she failed to build on the slopes of Mount Buderim would have had the houses stepped down the

Like Mawarra, Ardgarten descends the hill in a series of terraces

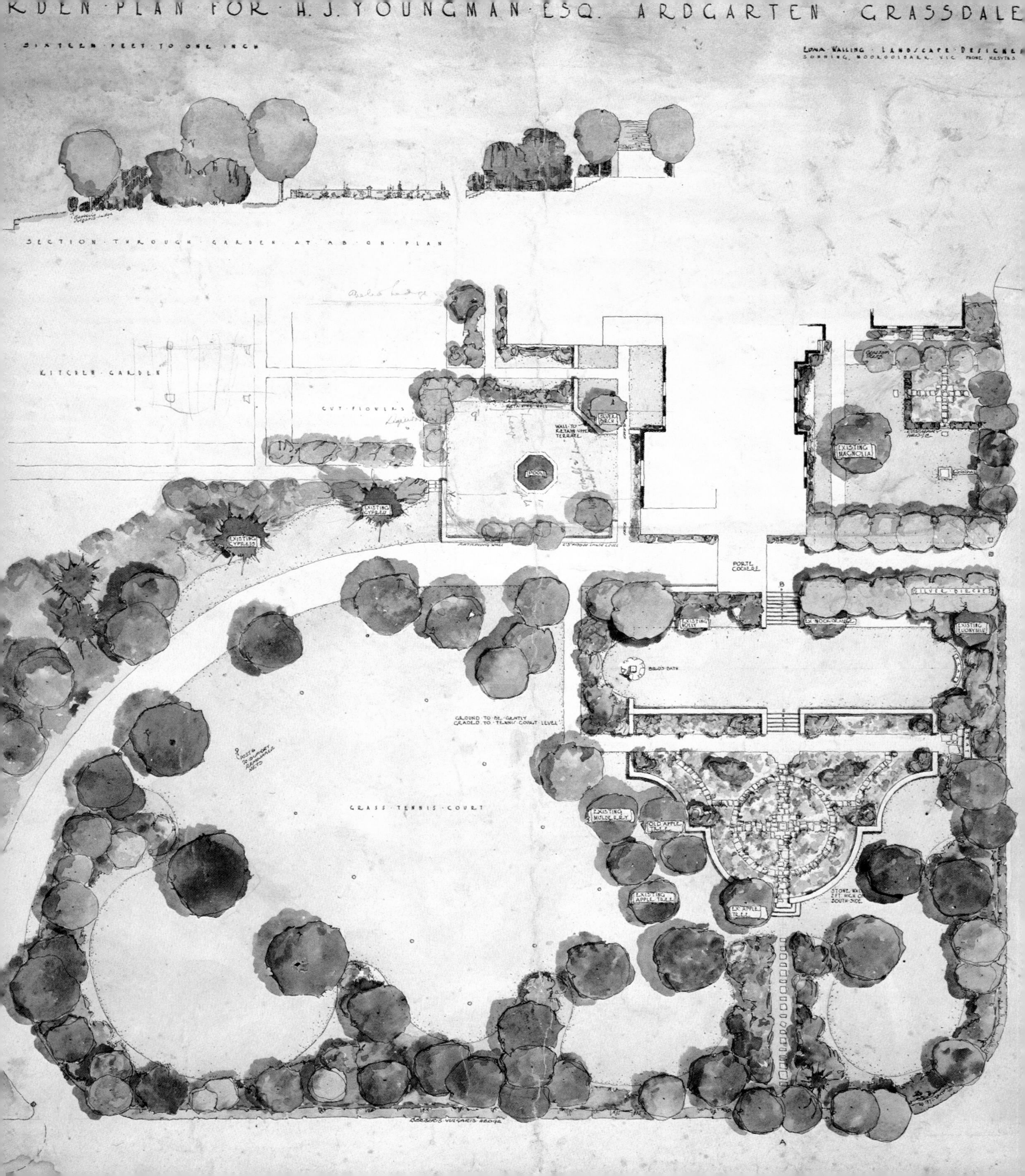

GARDEN PLAN FOR · H·J·YOUNGMAN·ESQ. ARDGARTEN · GRASSDALE

SIXTEEN FEET TO ONE INCH

EDNA WALLING · LANDSCAPE DESIGNER
SONNING, MOOROOLBARK, VIC. PHONE M.5573

SECTION · THROUGH · GARDEN · AT · AB · ON · PLAN

KITCHEN · GARDEN

CUT FLOWERS

POOL

WALL TO RETAIN UPPER TERRACE.

EXISTING CYPRESS

EXISTING CYPRESS

RETAINING WALL

PORTE COCHERE

GROUND TO BE GENTLY GRADED TO TENNIS COURT LEVEL

GRASS · TENNIS · COURT

EXISTING MAGNOLIA

EXISTING HOLLY

EXISTING MULBERRY

EXISTING APPLE TREE

EXISTING APPLE TREE

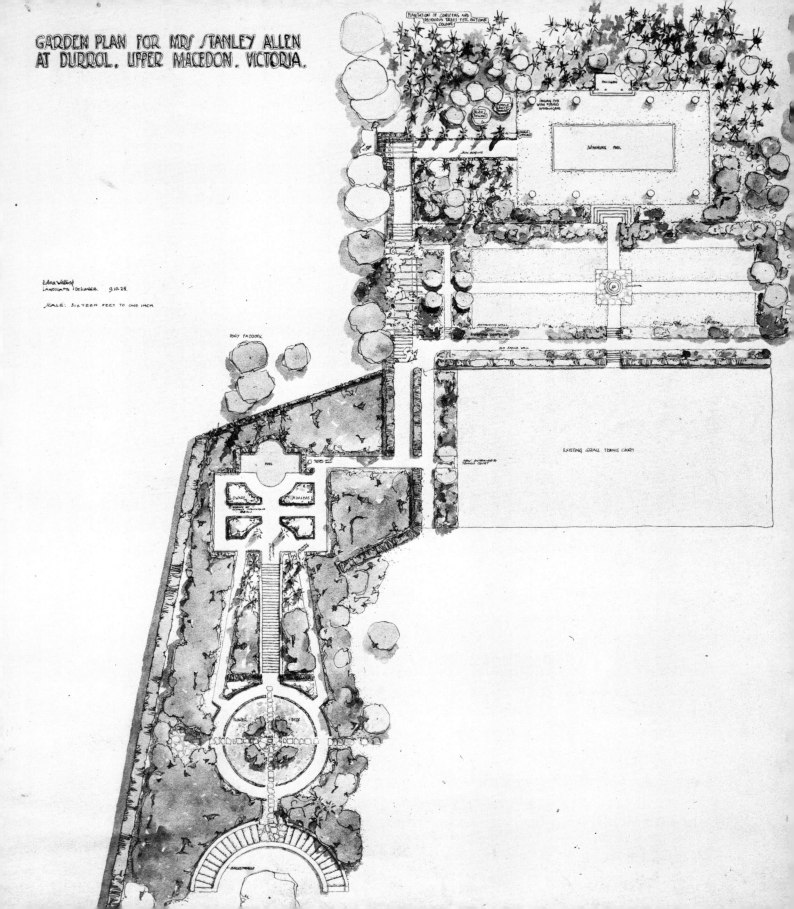

GARDEN PLAN FOR MRS STANLEY ALLEN
AT DURROL. UPPER MACEDON. VICTORIA.

Edna Walling
LANDSCAPE DESIGNER. 9.10.29.

SCALE: SIXTEEN FEET TO ONE INCH

PLANTATION OF CONIFERS AND DECIDUOUS TREES FOR AUTUMN COLOURS

SWIMMING POOL

PONY PADDOCK

DWARF AZALEAS

EXISTING GRASS TENNIS COURT

hill, connected by narrow winding walkways giving access to secluded courtyard gardens.

As early as 1925 she had designed an extension to the garden at 'Durrol', Mount Macedon, for Mrs Stanley Allen. It is pure Italianate in concept, descending a hill in a series of formal terraces, pools, ramps and stairs. The awkward shape of the site is masterfully handled by strong axes which tie the garden together.

Perhaps the best evidence of her interest in Italian gardens is 'Mawarra', a large garden she designed at Sherbrooke for the Misses Marshall and their sister Mrs McMillan in the early 1930s. Set in about 4 acres on a steeply sloping site, the garden

This plan of Durrol (incompletely carried out) shows Edna's skill at handling an awkward site

At Durrol, the formality of the principal axis descending the hill is barely discernible among the luxuriant growth of Mt Macedon

is laid out in a series of five terraces. They are designed as a 'nut walk', herbaceous border and birch walk. Edna Walling, who regarded Mawarra — or 'The Glades' as it was then known — as her finest work, described the garden herself in some unpublished notes entitled 'The Architecture of the Garden' as 'not so much a garden as a symphony in steps and beautiful trees'. In concept the garden is an imitation of the Italian Renaissance gardens such as the Villa d'Este, where a great central axis on the line of the principal room plunges down the slope, with side axes leading off along the contours.

Spanish gardens also held a special attraction for her, and she noted in *A Gardener's Log:*

For sheer restfulness, Spanish gardens, with their sheltered cloisters, sombre evergreens, paved courtyards, refreshing water features and climbing plants and pot plants (that supply colour with so little labour) seem much superior, much more serviceable, than Australian gardens as a whole.

It is really rather amazing that we have copies of the English style rather than Spanish and Italian, because in this climate protection from hot winds is so essential to intelligent living.

Here in Australia, quite intelligent people continue to live in houses that get hot enough to roast them.

Remarkably few have pergola covered out-of-doors living rooms. The majority have only two doors, so that to enter the garden you must go to the back door or the front door. Not to be able to bring the garden into the living room on a summer day would be intolerable to me.

To be able to walk out on to cool paving which has just been hosed down and to spread a cloth on a long low table under vines for a late evening meal is not a luxury: it is essential!

The other great influence on her work besides books on garden design was nature itself. 'Nothing can equal the exhilarating joy of those exquisite pieces of landscape in which the plant groups are still happily joined together', she wrote in the introduction to *The Australian Roadside.* The Australian landscape provided her with an endless source of inspiration. She saw beauty in the landscape, but she also understood the principles which governed it — why this tree grew in one location and not in another; why it grew in association with certain other species and so on.

Although for the first thirty-odd years of her professional life Walling used primarily exotic plant species, laws of nature she observed in the bush provided

The octagonal reflecting pool at Mawarra

valuable lessons in the principles of planting design. Whether the raw material was exotic or indigenous was of little consequence. Writing in *Gardens in Australia* in 1943 she notes that, following a trip to the country: 'All this will be stowed away in your mind ready to be recalled for inspiration . . .' But equally she could say: 'Really, for gate-crashing commend me to Foxgloves!' She delighted at the way such plants would, unaided, colonise a corner of the garden where they found suitable conditions. The plants had to survive with little or no assistance. If they died, then they were not suitable for that location. If they thrived, then one should plant more.

Commenting unfavourably in *A Gardener's Log* on a garden which had been laid out with regimented rows of trees, she says:

when you boil it all down this landscape gardening is chiefly a matter of observation. Walk along a country road . . . one that has not been meddled with, of course, and observe how nature groups her trees and shrubs; how many of the trees come right to the fore at times and some of the shrubs are right at the back. It is all so simple.

Walling's study of nature taught her a very natural approach to planting. To her the selection of 'plant material that will thrive quite happily under existing conditions is the whole secret of successful landscape gardening, and the first lesson to be learnt in planting is to create a natural setting for the growing of the more delicate gems within'.

Nature provided Edna Walling with both aesthetic and scientific lessons, and she made the most of both.

Edna Walling frequently photographed the countryside from which she drew so much inspiration

CHAPTER THREE:
TRADEMARKS &
SIGNATURE TUNES

Apart from Edna Walling's conversion to Australian plants in the 1950s, she showed no apparent stylistic development of any real consequence during her career. From the beginning she appears to have possessed a confident and personal style that she found little need to change over forty years.

Some of the design drawings dating from the early 1920s lack the confidence and fluidity of later drawings. The gardens tend to be very formal, and the arrangement of the various elements is not particularly well disposed. One can almost see the designer poring over part of the plan but forgetting the total concept. It is possible that some of the less fluid drawings and designs are the work of associates, although they appear to be in Walling's hand. There are many drawings from these early years, however, that show both confidence and excellence of design. By the late 1920s this was the case with all of them. For her clients Edna would often prepare an exquisitely rendered water-colour sketch on hand-made Whatman paper. These were executed with a combination of great boldness and delicacy, and were apparently dashed off in a few hours each. Simple blueprints were used for contractors and on-site supervision.

Edna's soft, informal style of planting is retained in the Marshall garden today

But by the mid-1950s her rough pencil drawings on brown paper (see page 33) were intended to give only a broad outline of the proposed work. Unfortunately none of the pencil sketches seem to have survived and it is not therefore possible to analyse any small changes in style at this time. It seems fairly certain, however, that most of the formal elements — walls, large flights of stairs, pergolas and the like — were used less frequently in the interests of a more natural native garden.

Although Edna's style changed so little over the years, she nevertheless produced, through this period, gardens of quite varied character. They do not fall into clearly defined categories. Rather, each usually contains some of the characteristics of the others. Walling recognised that different styles of architecture and different allotment sizes demanded different forms of garden design. In an article in the *Australian Home Beautiful* in 1926 she said:

It seems a pity that some of the things that attract us so much in old world cottage gardens have been applied to villas and mansions, where they look as awkward as would the cotter invited to take tea in the drawing room of one whose station in life he readily acknowledges to be higher than his own . . . how often we see extensive grounds where one expected the quiet dignity of big trees and well grouped shrubs bordering a lawn of graceful undulations,

In one of Edna's early drawings her use of shading, notes and small elevational sketches make it possible to visualise the finished garden

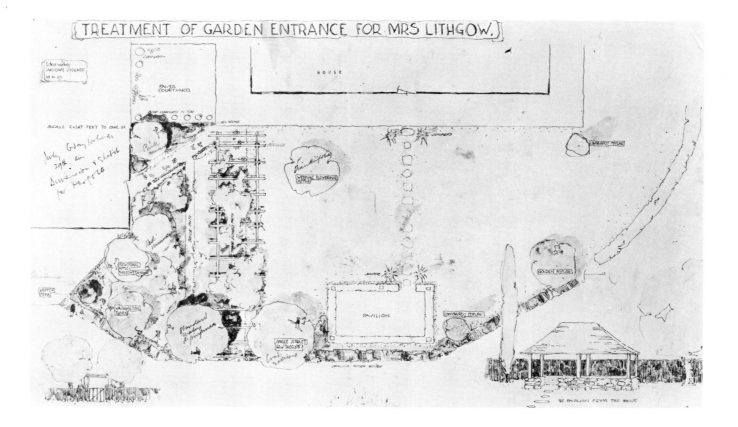

presenting nothing but a dazzling mass of flowers with a few shrubs and trees so subordinate to them as to be almost negligible.

GARDEN STYLES   Three main categories of style may be identified in Edna Walling's work: informal cottage, structured, and formal geometric.

Informal cottage gardens surrounded the cottages at Bickleigh Vale village. Unfortunately only a few of them, especially 'Lynton Lee' and 'Glencairn', retain their original character in 1991. So delicate and personal are these cottage gardens that they will not survive without a gentle caring hand continually guiding them. The loss of most of the Bickleigh Vale gardens is regrettable but Walling's first two books, *Gardens in Australia* and *Cottage and Garden in Australia,* give an excellent impression of these gardens and their underlying philosophy.

Basically they were gardens for gardeners. No elaborate plans were prepared and the gardens grew according to the whims of their owners — under the guidance of Walling, of course. They were 'the sort of garden in which you could garden if you wanted to but if you didn't it would not matter', as she said in *A Gardener's Log*. She described cottage gardens in *Cottage and Garden in Australia*:

There is no formality, nothing stereotyped, not the slightest thing to recall the rather self-conscious gardens of the suburbs with the same proportion of lawn (never more than a week long) and the same well trimmed hedge; for here in the cottage garden the picture develops by 'slip' and cutting, by root and seed, brought in a neighbour's basket and poked into some quickly stirred up patch of soil which happens to be unoccupied.

Edna Walling was responsible for the basic layout of those cottage gardens and their main planting, the latter being supplied from the Sonning nursery. The owners were then encouraged to add plants of all sorts wherever there was a place and allow 'the self-sown foxgloves, cynoglossums, columbines, sweet williams and forget-me-nots to fight it out among themselves'. These gardens were spontaneous but not haphazard. Walling would never have allowed that.

Stone paths and terraces were softened with self-sown plants. Thyme lawns were scythed in gradations between short and long to blend one area into another. Dry-stone walls and pergolas clothed with flowers, sweeping lawns and small pools were all part of these gardens. Trees were planted in copses on the lawns and shrub

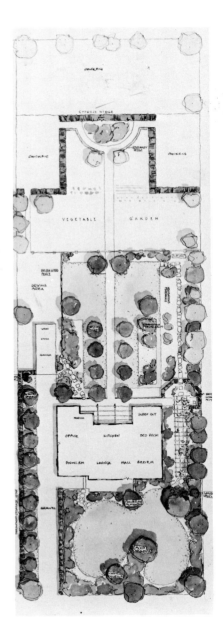

The garden designed for the Gellie family was a typically 'structured' one: informal at the front but axial and geometric behind the house

beds densely planted, but without excluding any self-sown perennial which happened to take a fancy to a particular spot. Bulbs were sprinkled through the lawn in drifts, with concentrations around trees, and altogether the cottages and their gardens took on the appearance of many of the snug little cottages in the southwest of England.

'Structured' gardens are most often associated with houses on a typical quarter- to half-acre suburban allotment but were also used for many country gardens, although on a grander scale in such cases. They are gardens that successfully achieved a happy blend of the cottage and the geometric styles.

Structured gardens are generally divided into separate compartments, each with its own character. Edna Walling was expert at integrating different compartments, and her skilful design meant that it was possible to slip happily from one area into another. The garden shown on page 70 is an excellent demonstration of Walling's skill in successfully coping with difficult junctions resulting from an oddly shaped site. Often on a suburban allotment the front garden became the 'cottage' garden, with dense planting in sweeping beds around the perimeter, stone paths to the front door, and large specimen trees and copses of trees in the lawns. Although both the plans of these front gardens and the surviving gardens themselves appear to be casual and informal, they nevertheless are cleverly contrived. The small allotments have enabled the designer to exploit fully her talent for false perspective. These small gardens seem far larger than they are and the eye is led on through what is a seemingly endless series of pictures.

The rear garden might be more formally laid out on a rigid axis or axes and dominated by the architectural forms of walls, pergolas, steps, colonnades and formally shaped pools. The planting was relied on to soften the structure and geometry of the layout. The garden Edna Walling designed at 'Yathong' for Mrs H. Ledger in the mid-1920s survives as an early, though modified, example of this style. So too does the garden designed for Mrs L.B. Marshall

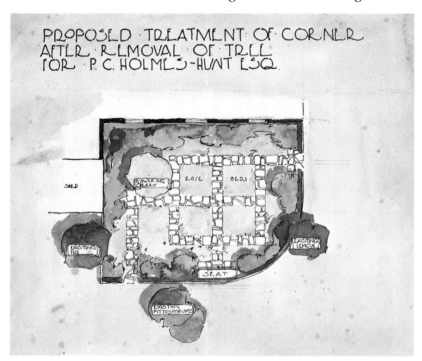

PROPOSED · TREATMENT · OF · CORNER
AFTER · REMOVAL · OF · TREE
FOR · P. C. HOLMES-HUNT ESQ.

PLAN OF GARDEN FOR F. GRASSICK ESQ. HEIDELBERG

FOR MRS H. LEDGER, CHURCH STREET · BENALLA · VICTORIA.

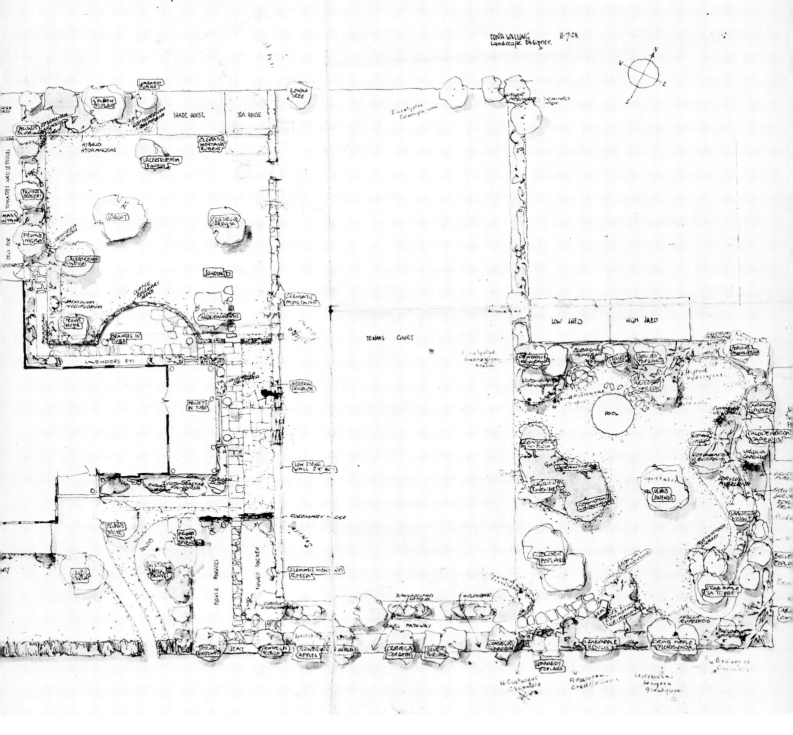

EDNA WALLING
Landscape Designer.   11·7·28.

at Ivanhoe (page 104), although in this case the rear garden has the same informality as the front.

The 'formal geometric' gardens are generally associated with grand houses on large allotments. During the late 1920s and through the 1930s many of these were laid out in the more affluent Melbourne suburbs, using the cheap labour available during the Depression and its aftermath.

The gardens are characteristically geometric in design, sometimes rigidly so. Major formal elements such as swimming pools, pergolas, decorative pools, tennis courts, terrace walls and colonnades are beautifully tied together by axial paths that intersect at critical locations in the design. These paths may incorporate a massive flight of stairs or curving ramps such as those at 'Mawarra', Sherbrooke (page 65). The paths are often lined with herbaceous borders or clipped hedges, and paved terraces and rock walls are used extensively. In fact these gardens gave Walling the opportunity to indulge her passion for rockwork and architectural gardens on a grand scale. Indeed the rockwork at Mawarra is said to have cost £2000 which, if one considers mid-1920s values, gives some idea of its extent.

The Toorak garden designed for Dr Ringland Anderson in 1934 is perhaps the most rigidly geometric of all Edna Walling's designs. The swimming pool, pergolas, tennis courts and herbaceous borders are mirror-imaged along a central axis. In typical Walling style, however, there was an area designated, à la Robinson, as the 'wild garden'.

These formal gardens, like the merely 'structured' ones, are able to combine a number of disparate elements happily and restfully into an integrated whole. This was one of Edna Walling's outstanding talents. The other striking aspect of these formal gardens is their detailing and proportion. This is nowhere better demonstrated than at Mawarra, where these features are flawless and the design of the main structural elements disarmingly simple.

The garden at Yathong, designed for Mrs H. Ledger, is divided into rectangular compartments. A low stone wall and colonnade separate the terrace from a tennis lawn and 'wild garden', seen through a gap in the wall

Part of the wall at Yathong supports a simple wistaria-clad colonnade framing various views

Formal gardens of this kind were softened by Edna's characteristic magical veil of planting. Rock walls are trailed with clematis; erigeron thrives between paving-stones and in crevices on stairs. Perennials are allowed to 'escape' happily from herbaceous borders, and overhead are the canopies of birch, prunus, ash and the other typical Walling plants. As she says in *A Gardener's Log*,

It is understandable that there is so much abhorrence of the formal garden for so exquisite in proportion and line must the design be that we very rarely see an example that is likely to move one to admiration. Then again, the planting of a formal garden can utterly ruin it. This is one of the most difficult tasks, for to be a success the planting should be mostly in-formal, so that it becomes the softening influence that is so necessary to the formal design.

Edna Walling's strong design philosophy embraced a wide and consistent reper-toire. But her repetitive use of standard details never led to a sameness of design, a criticism often levelled at designers — architects and engineers as well as landscape designers. Walling observed a number of general principles and within these al-lowed herself considerable flexibility.

STRUCTURE AND ARCHITECTURAL DESIGN   'Once the walls, stairways and terraces were completed the planting had to be faced, of course, and I was sufficiently in-terested in my new gardens not to have spoilt them by planting that I did not like.

Always I longed for a collaborator to whom I could hand over this side of the planting work while I got on with more building of gardens.' [Unpublished notes]

Walling believed that a strong underly-ing architectural design was necessary in gardens, except those around cottages. The need for this, she thought, became greater as the size of the garden became smaller. The unification of house and garden was one of her greatest interests and this she achieved by linking the house with the main axes in the garden and by extending the house into the garden with the aid

This very formal garden was designed for Dr Ringland Anderson in 1934. Although the garden has changed through subdivision the fine entry gates and piers still remain

THE GARDEN PLAN FOR MRS RINGLAND ANDERSON, TOORAK.

of pergolas, low stone walls, piazzas and other architectural devices. She also recognised that in a formal garden the beauty of its architectural form would survive even if the garden was allowed to get out of hand, perhaps by a subsequent owner. She had seen and noted in *A Gardener's Log* 'how much of Guilfoyle's work had been cramped, instead of being developed, through the slaughtering of material with which he built up his pictures . . .'

The formal garden, as she saw it, also had the advantage of retaining its charm in winter. As she also said in *A Gardener's Log*,

When the design is good the winter garden has a charm equal to its summer effect; but when it is inferior one must look forward to winter with a certain measure of dread, when all the defects of the design that summer growth and colour have so kindly veiled are revealed . . .

PERSPECTIVE AND DECEPTION 'In a small garden we must rely on deception a great deal. If the borders are allowed to sweep well out into the lawn in places . . . the whole of the garden will not be visible immediately one enters the gateway, and a visitor will experience interest and surprise at the seeming extent of the garden.' [*Australian Home Beautiful*, 1926]

This was a principle used frequently in many of Walling's gardens where the front of the house was designed in a natural manner allowing for this sort of treatment, while the back garden was more formal. The effect was achieved by planting out the boundaries very densely, except where a distant view, or nearby foliage, could be exposed to give a greater sense of distance. These dense planting beds were scooped into the lawn to break up its geometry, and clumps of trees were planted along the line of view to give a feeling of distance created by looking through a screen of tree trunks. Birches were the most commonly used trees for this purpose and the garden at 'Wooleen' in Benalla, designed for Mrs L. Ledger in the late

The garden for Dr Ringland Anderson combined both the formal and natural styles

1930s, demonstrates today the wonderful sense of space and distance created on a relatively small allotment. Walling also exploited the characteristics of her planting to give a greater sense of distance. As she said in *A Gardener's Log*,

Not only the actual dimensions of the whole plant, but the size of the foliage is a point, too; big leaves tend to bring the plant closer to the observer, thus reducing the apparent extent of the garden. And so you see that by using plants with small foliage, you give a texture to the pattern of your garden that tends to enlarge it and to create a greater sense of distance.

Walling loathed a garden which could be taken in at a glance. Her gardens are ones where there is a new discovery on every visit, no matter how frequently made.

CREATING PICTURES AND NATURAL EFFECTS   'A garden should, I always feel, be just a little too big to keep the whole cultivated, then it has a chance to go a little wild in spots and make some pictures for you . . . Confronted with several acres to be planted we always seem to be at somewhat of a loss, and frequently end up by dressing up the whole area with specimen trees and lawn, and it is so frightfully

Wooleen's garden, just around the corner from Yathong, is smaller and less formal: details of the planting have been planned with great care

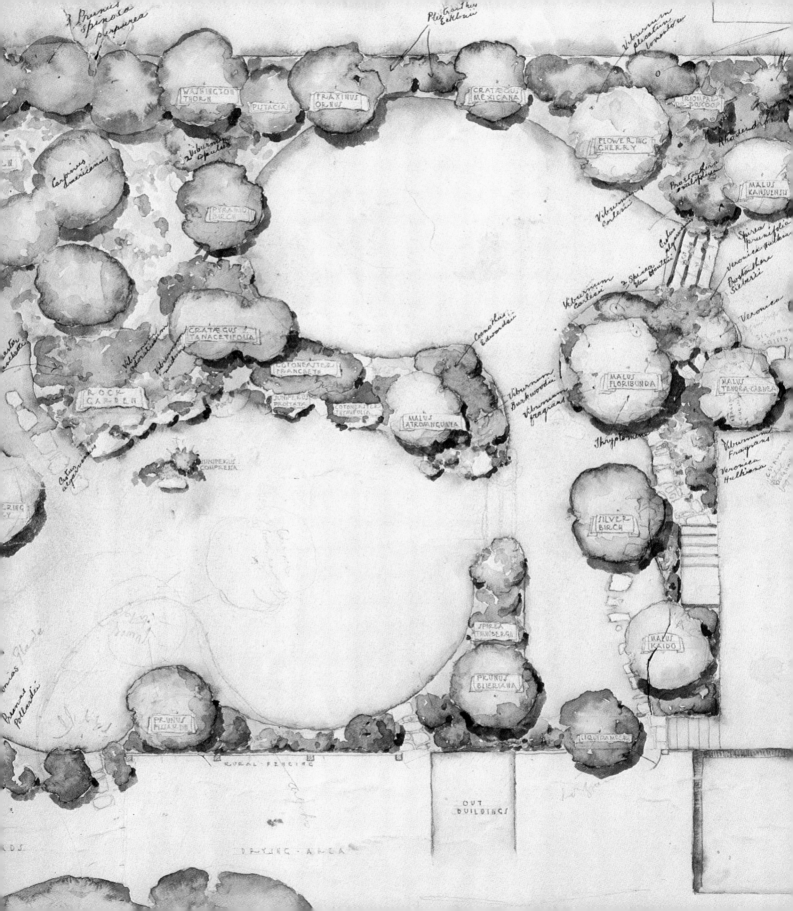

3 Prunus
Spinosa
purpurea

Plectranthus
Eckhieri

Viburnum
plicatum tomentosum

WASHINGTON
THORN

PISTACIA

FRAXINUS
ORNUS

CRATÆGUS
MEXICANA

TRIUMPHALE
DE BOSCOOP

2 Viburnum
opulus

FLOWERING
CHERRY

Rhododendron

Carpinus
americanus

MALUS
KANSUENSIS

PYRAMID
BIRCH

Prostanthera
rotundifolia

Viburnum
Carlesii

Spirea
prunifolia

Veronica pulkerr

Prostanthera
Sieberii

Veronica

Viburnum
Carlesii

2 Spirea
Van Houttei

Ceanothus
Edwardsii

CRATÆGUS
TANACETIFOLIA

Cydonia
alpina

COTONEASTER
FRANCHETI

Viburnum
tomentosum

Viburnum

Cistus
purpureus

Viburnum
Burkwoodii

Viburnum
fragrans

MALUS
FLORIBUNDA

MALUS
TENORA-CÆRULEA

ROCK
GARDEN

JUNIPERUS
PROSTRATA

Po.

COTONEASTER
TRYMIFOLIA

MALUS
ATROSANGUINEA

Cotoneaster
microphylla

Crataegus
oxyacantha

JUNIPERUS
COMPRESSA

Thryptomene

Viburnum
Fragrans

Veronica
Hulkiana

MALUS
FLORIBUNDA

FLOWER
ING
Y

SILVER
BIRCH

Prunus glauca

Prunus
pollardii

SPIREA
THUNBERGII

MALUS
KAIDO

PRUNUS
BLIREIANA

PRUNUS
PISSARDII

LIQUIDAMBAR

RURAL FENCING

OUT
BUILDINGS

DRYING AREA

dull. To be able to wander off into a little forest somewhere would be much more romantic, and if we can't be romantic in the development of our gardens we might as well be dead.' [*A Gardener's Log*]

It is in Edna Walling's notion of landscape pictures that she shows herself to be a passionate and incurable romantic. Like Gertrude Jekyll she developed a concept of the garden as a series of 'pictures' as one moved about it. A view through a colonnade, along a vista, through a window or into a corner of carefully designed planting gave opportunities to create individual pictures. They were the soft, dappled paintings of Monet, Renoir and Heysen, not the starker, more angular works of her own generation. Walling constantly strove to make a series of harmonious pictures, and in *Gardens in Australia* gave planting proposals for different times of year which 'are . . . suggestions given to encourage individuals to create their own garden pictures'. These garden pictures were, as individual set pieces, a work of art. But they were ever-changing pictures as well as static ones. A walk through a Walling garden was a series of constantly unfolding discoveries, as she described it in *Gardens in Australia*:

A drift of primroses under an apple tree; a lonely flat boulder half submerged under Westmoreland thyme; a turn in a glade that brings them face to face with a lovely tree in all its autumn glory, and the shimmering effects of pools.

COLONNADES AND PERGOLAS   'There are few more charming ways of separating one part of the garden from another than by a colonnade, more especially when the need is for something that divides rather than conceals another part of the garden.' [*Australian Home Beautiful*, 1934]

Walling used this device especially where relief was needed in a flat garden. The colonnade was generally built on top of a low stone wall or on free-standing pillars with a low hedge between. The structure, both wall and superstructure, was planted with trailing creepers. Colonnades exactly suited Walling's concept of garden pictures. She wrote in the *Australian Home Beautiful* in 1934: 'It is most interesting to note the extensive effects that can be created with a colonnade, through the columns of which one catches pictures of the garden beyond.'

Similarly with pergolas: they helped to create pictures and they divided the garden. Walling often used them to frame a door or the window of the principal room.

In 1937 the owner of Boortkoi asked Edna to extend a garden she had already completed by designing this pergola as a wedding anniversary gift for his wife. The superstructure of saplings covered with wistaria is supported on roughly plastered rubble columns

Her pergolas were generally free-standing, but nearly always related to the house or some other structure. Sometimes a retaining wall or the fence around a service area formed one side of the pergola. Like the colonnades her pergolas were generally built of plastered rubble columns or exposed stone piers. Unlike the colonnades, which were capped with dressed timbers, they usually had a superstructure of saplings. These structures could be very extensive and it was not uncommon for a design to incorporate a pergola 80 to 100 feet long.

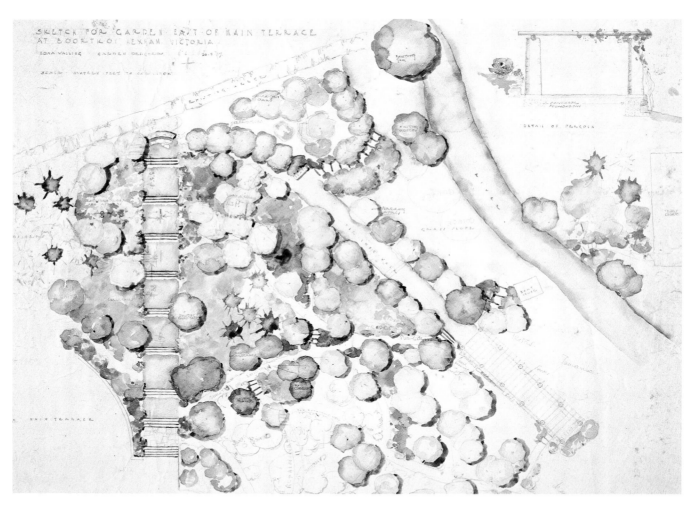

The Boortkoi pergola covers part of 'the long walk', a flat, grassy terrace overlooking a river. The garden behind is informally planted with almonds, mulberries, hawthorns and other flowering trees. In the original plan this area was designated 'kitchen garden'

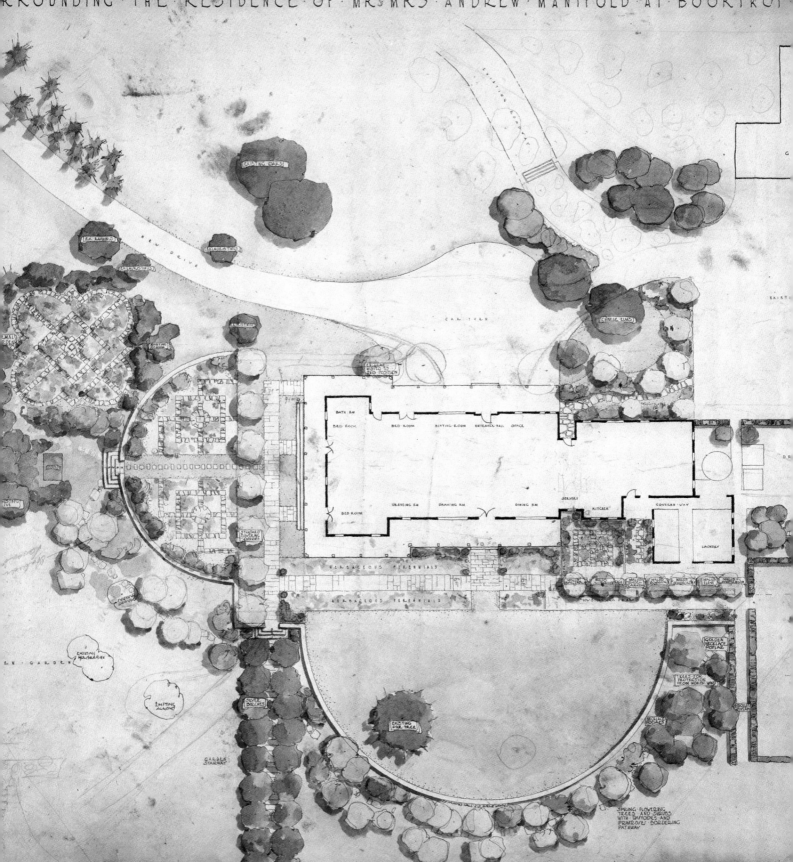

BALUSTRADES   'The balustrade is a form of garden construction that gives more dignity and more delicacy of line than does any other form of construction.' [*A Gardener's Log*]

Ironically, Walling rarely used any form of balustrading as such. Occasionally wrought iron was used, but more often the edge of a terrace was simply a low stone

The formal geometric terraces at Ardgarten contrast with the more natural parts of the garden they overlook. The plan for this garden is on page 69

wall. She greatly admired the patterns of European balustrades, considering it 'unwise to depart from them, since they have stood the test of centuries . . . ' Perhaps the reason she did not use this device more often was that the qualities she admired so much could not be matched by local tradesmen, nor were the Australian gardens extensive enough to use the balustrade form with the boldness it demanded.

PROPORTION AND SCALE   'There can scarcely be any hard and fast rules about dimensions and proportions, for rarely, if ever, are two sets of conditions alike; so much depends upon the size of the garden, the position the pergola is to occupy, and the architecture of the house, therefore it is necessary to stress the care which must be taken to ensure that the scale and proportion is right before erecting such features.' [*Gardens in Australia*]

There is little that can be added to this except to say that Walling, in her own work, shows a total mastery of both proportion and scale. Whether she is organising a new garden around a large country house, or detailing the end of a stone wall or flight of steps, her proportions are superb. On occasions when an unlimited budget would be likely to tempt others to extravagance, she showed total restraint.

SIMPLICITY   'There should be intellectual enjoyment as well as emotional pleasure in the contemplation of our gardens, and this will come only with good but simple design.' [*A Gardener's Log*]

It might be thought by some that, in comparison with native gardens devoid of all extraneous decoration, Walling's colonnaded and walled gardens are far from simple. And perhaps they are right, for a native garden associated with the right house may not require any embellishment. But in the 1920s Walling's gardens with their rustic elegance were hardly the norm. Many of the plans themselves, despite their formality, and sometimes even complexity, were essentially simple in concept. Had they not been they would never have achieved their disarmingly restful qualities. The structural elements — pergolas, stone walls, stairways and the like — were not laboured in detail. Their excellent proportions and simple detailing gave them enough character. Compared with the average garden at the time with its crazy paving, standard roses, clipped shrubs and neatly edged beds, Walling's gardens were the essence of simplicity.

EXPLOITING LEVELS 'How important it is to take advantage of anything unusual about the site', wrote Edna Walling in *Gardens in Australia*. Nothing gave her greater pleasure than designing a garden that allowed her to give vent to her flair for dealing with changing levels. Whether it was the garden at Mawarra, with its great flights of steps, ramps and terraces or a garden with one simple broad step, she used the natural slope of a site to advantage. Her work at Mawarra was perhaps the grandest exploitation of levels she achieved, and she always regarded it as her finest design.

Changing levels gave her an opportunity to use the architectural elements she enjoyed so much. High retaining walls were ideal for supporting one side of a pergola, and ramps and steps could be used to negotiate steep rises. Invariably part of a sloping site was allowed to retain its natural contours, for she abhorred the completely terraced gardens that were so fashionable in the 1930s in Melbourne.

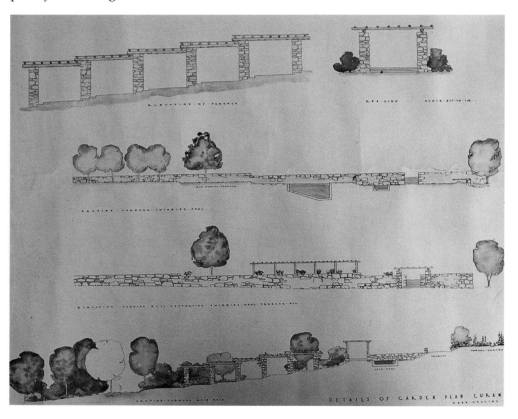

For this large country garden, Eurambeen, Edna Walling designed a formal terrace around an existing pool. The interlocking stone walls, terraces and pergolas show her mastery of difficult, sloping sites

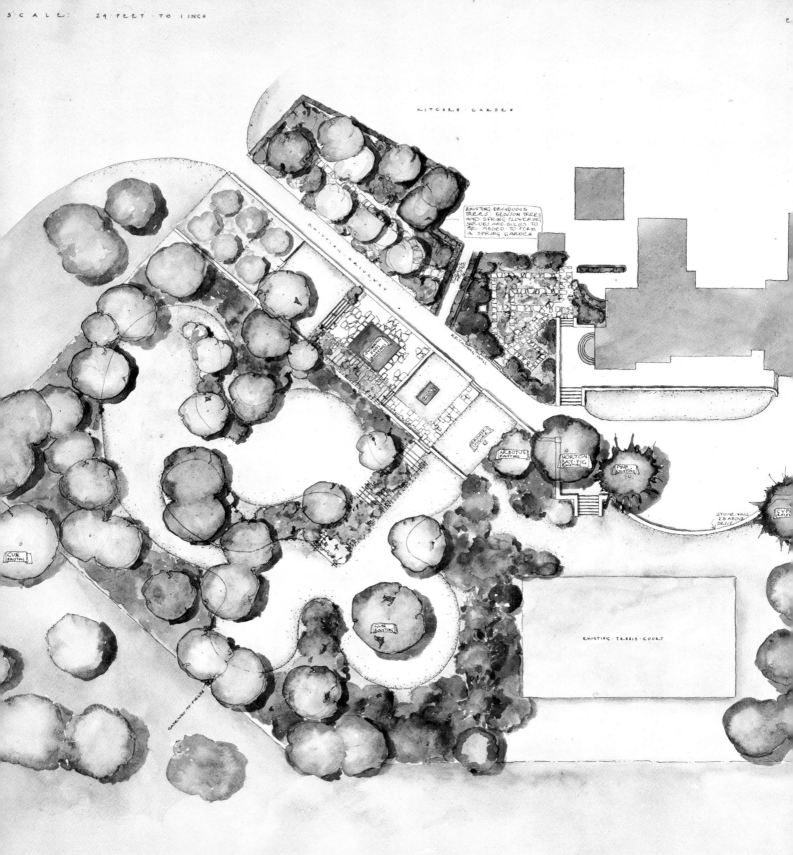

KITCHEN · GARDEN

EXISTING DECIDUOUS
TREES: BLOSSOM TREES
AND SPRING FLOWERING
SHRUBS AND BULBS TO
BE ADDED TO FORM
A SPRING GARDEN

EXISTING DRIVEWAY

RETAINING WALL

BASIN

ABOVE
PERGOLA

ARBUTUS
EXISTING

MORTON
BAY FIG
EXISTING

PINE
EXISTING

STONE WALL
IS ABOVE DRIVE

CYP
EXIST

GUM
EXISTING

GUM
EXISTING

GATEWAY TO FIELDS

EXISTING · TENNIS · COURT

STEPS AND RAMPS 'Steps and stairways! What delightful fancies with which to idly play. What could be more romantic than a formal garden stairway or more intriguing than brief steps of boulders? And with what precision and care these things must be designed . . .' [*Gardens in Australia*]

In Walling's gardens, steps not only served the practical purpose of giving access to different levels but were an aesthetic feature of no mean importance. Her steps were as varied as her gardens, although she did have a number of favourite styles. In a formal setting the steps, nearly always of stone, had an overhang of an inch or so. In less formal situations the steps were invariably without an overhang or

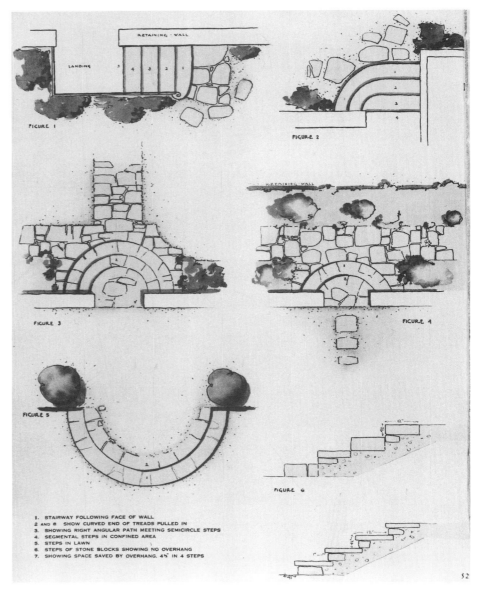

1. STAIRWAY FOLLOWING FACE OF WALL
2 AND 8 SHOW CURVED END OF TREADS PULLED IN
3. SHOWING RIGHT ANGULAR PATH MEETING SEMICIRCLE STEPS
4. SEGMENTAL STEPS IN CONFINED AREA
5. STEPS IN LAWN
6. STEPS OF STONE BLOCKS SHOWING NO OVERHANG
7. SHOWING SPACE SAVED BY OVERHANG. 4½" IN 4 STEPS

These sketches of steps, drawn by Edna, were published in Gardens in Australia *in 1943*

52

were made of casually placed boulders. Her steps were beautifully proportioned, generally with treads of 12 inches and risers of 4½ inches. She used semi-circular steps, a form also favoured by Jekyll, but with great restraint, recognising that where the change in level required more than about three steps this form was not appropriate.

In a number of her gardens Walling used curving ramps. These are an intriguing and unusual device which she designed with great care. Invariably two ramps were used about a central axis. The ramps at Mawarra she described as 'actually a series of gravel areas sloping to narrow stone steps only 3 inches high and thus very easily negotiated'. They were not as easy to construct, as Eric Hammond readily remembers. The stone walls that form balustrades on either side are a tortuous piece of construction, not only descending but curving as they go. Nevertheless this is an impressive piece of design and construction, which has stood solidly for fifty years.

WATERING 'A well mulched garden will stand up to a great deal of heat before it requires watering, if at all, and watering should *never* be started before it is absolutely necessary, for once you start, the resistance of the plants is weakened, and they no longer survive without this artificial aid.' [*Gardens in Australia*]

It is surprising to many that the gardens Walling designed at Bickleigh Vale, using essentially exotic plants, were usually supplied with only one tap per acre. This principle of one tap per acre was a real constraint on Walling's designs and is probably a major reason why she developed such a strong ecological bias. The majority of the plants she used, if properly mulched and cared for, did not require the massive watering they often received as soon as her back was turned. She condemned the wastage of water resulting each year from unnecessary watering of gardens, and she promoted proper horticultural methods to reduce this need.

POOLS 'Pools and other water features have become so popular that no persuasive words are needed to induce owners to install them in their gardens.' [*A Gardener's Log*]

Walling certainly needed no persuasion to use water features in gardens she designed. There can hardly be any of her designs that do not incorporate water somewhere, and such features varied greatly. They could be of the most formal

This swimming pool, built for Miss Hughes-Jones in 1939–40, was the result of a collaboration between Edna Walling and Ellis Stones. Both claimed credit for it. Built of stone and rendered in cement, it was a remarkable piece of design and construction

kind, or the most natural and casual of ponds. Often her pools were simple rectangular or quatrefoil shapes with a stone coping about 12 to 18 inches wide set flush with the lawn. Occasionally a formal, slightly raised pool, with a similar coping, was placed against a high retaining wall incorporating a simple wall fountain. If a fountain was used it was more often a single jet of water placed centrally in the pool.

Her casual pools ranged in size from a few feet across to large swimming pools. They were generally well set with boulders. One of Walling's greatest pieces of design was a swimming pool built for Miss E. Hughes-Jones at Olinda. It was constructed by Ellis Stones in 1939 and, although now modified, remains an outstanding achievement by two great designers acting in collaboration. If garden history is given new directions by great individual works, then this beautifully natural pool is a major pivot in Australian garden design.

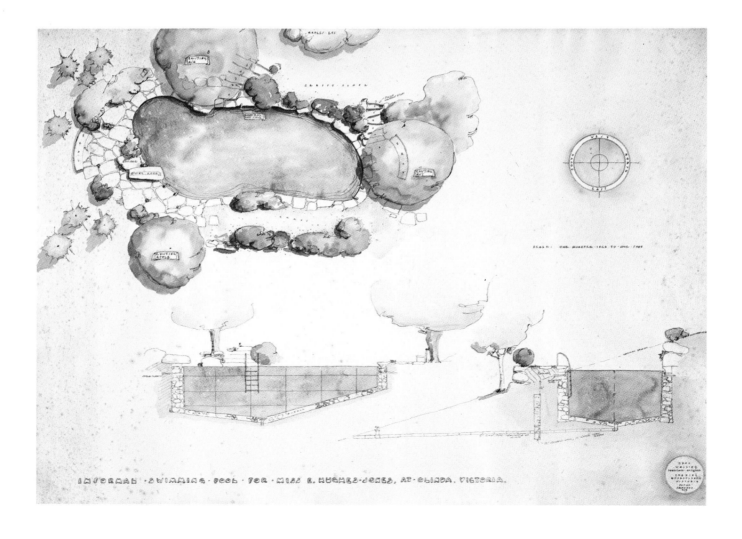

MATERIALS 'It is interesting to note that sometimes even when the materials employed are good, results can be disappointing . . .' [*Gardens in Australia*]

Walling used a very limited repertoire of materials. She would not tolerate concrete, although she did use it occasionally for small irregular stepping-stones when no other material was readily available. She preferred the natural materials, but always in the hands of expert craftsmen. Walls were invariably of stone; paving of stone or brick; driveways of flagstones or crushed limestone; and pergolas of stone piers with saplings for the superstructure. She had a great liking for hand-wrought iron (see page 35), which she considered gave 'an opportunity of expressing design with a lightness not easily obtained with other material'.

Decorative elements were welcome in the garden, but were only included with the utmost restraint. She considered that sculpture, used well, could 'embroider a part of the garden with an emotion as well as a decoration'. Flower pots, she felt, could be used more liberally, and her cottage gardens were dotted with her own hand-made coloured and patterned cement pots. Wooden casks bulging with hydrangeas or clipped yews suited more formal situations and were used frequently.

DRIVEWAYS AND PATHWAYS 'Above all places the driveway is one where the greatest restraint will be exercised, for it is so desirable that it should be entirely presentable and pleasing at all times of the year.' [*Gardens in Australia*]

'Paved pathways trickling up to the front door are very inviting, and when they are laid with not too much care as to line they are much more charming than when they follow a perfect curve.' [*A Gardener's Log*]

Walling observed one very strict rule about both her paths and driveways. If they were of necessity straight or formal, then they were very straight. If not they were the reverse, with an understated naturalness. Her driveways were generally of limestone toppings, but occasionally of stone paving where a more formal treatment was required. Paths varied from brick, which were always straight, to stepping-stones, but her favoured type was a narrow track winding through the garden 'just sprinkled with gritty sand or inconspicuous gravel'.

She noted in *A Gardener's Log* that 'Expensively laid pathways are nearly always ugly!' And added: 'Isn't that encouraging?' She loathed any form of plinth, regarding them as 'all expensive and all ugly'. Small plants were encouraged to

Published in Australian Home Beautiful, *the entrance to the garden of Mrs E. J. Rowse. The wall in the background supports posts and a beam for climbing plants, and divides the driveway from the garden*

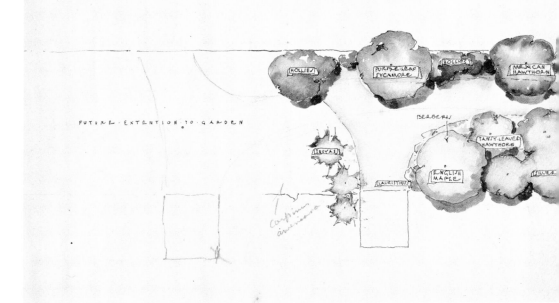

FUTURE·EXTENTION·TO·GARDEN

HOLLIES

PURPLE·LEAF·SYCAMORE

HOLLIES

MEXICAN·HAWTHORN

BERBERIS

AZUKAS

TANSY·LEAVED·HAWTHORN

LAURESTINUS

ENGLISH·MAPLE

SILVER

carpinus americana

The plan for Folly Farm's driveway

A garden designed for the Marshall family in Ivanhoe, Victoria

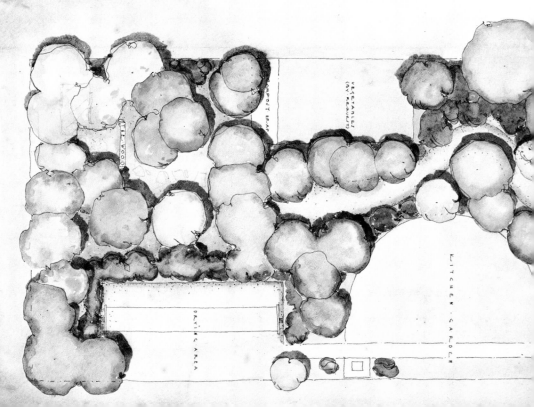

THE · GARDEN · PLAN · FOR · MRS · L.B.

SCALE · TEN FEET · TO · ONE

COMPOST·HEAP

VEGETABLES (IN SEASON)

SILVER·WOOD

DRYING·AREA

KITCHEN·GARDEN

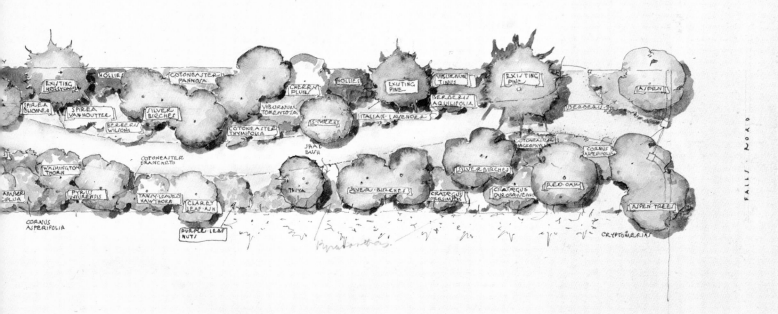

ESTED · PLANTING · OF · ROADWAY · FOR · DR · L. B. COX, OLINDA.

EDNA WALLING GARDEN DESIGNER.

HALL · AT · HEIDLEBERG.

EDNA · WALLING · GARDEN · DESIGNER.

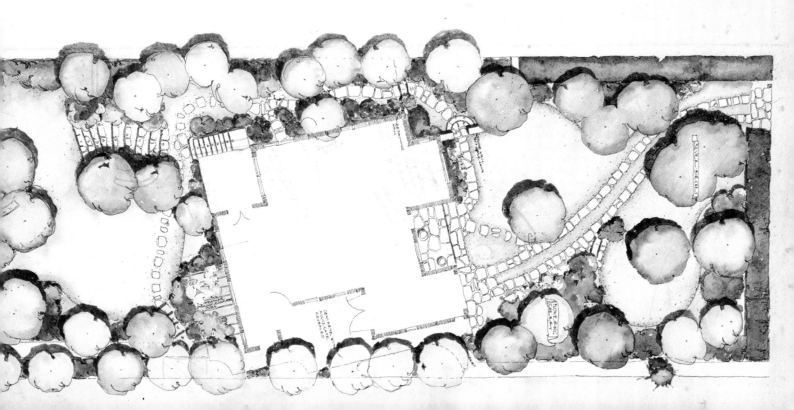

invade paths and driveways to soften their edges. 'They do no harm and will form a much prettier edge than that meticulous curve or a perfect straight line . . .'

ROCKS AND BOULDERS   'I have found that in landscape gardening a few weathered boulders, especially those that are large and somewhat flat, will give stability to a design that might otherwise be rather dull.' [*A Gardener's Log*]

One cannot be sure whether Edna Walling's concept of a natural rock outcrop, or that of Ellis Stones, came first. Whichever way it was, Stones was most certainly responsible for constructing all Edna's significant rock outcrops — even to the point of placing the boulders in Edna's own garden. She understood all the principles, but was happy to leave the actual work in the hands of a master craftsman.

Edna's outdoor kitchen used during the construction of her cottage at East Point, near Lorne

WALLS 'Low stone walls when simply constructed are always charming. Any
elaboration in the form of "tuck pointing"or the use of spectacular stone, or even
worse, a variety of stones, such as sandstone and marble — to use an exaggerated
illustration, gives an eccentric effect.' [*Gardens in Australia*]

Edna Walling was sometimes teased by her friends because of her passion for building walls. Low stone walls could fairly be described as her main trademark, so widely
did she use them. Not that they were used just for the sake of it. Walling used walls
essentially for two purposes. The first was to retain the soil on a sloping site, and
the second was to relieve the flatness of a site that was without the benefit of any
natural slopes or undulations. In the latter instance the walls were often combined
with colonnades to form a vertical screen, thus dividing the garden into different
sections.

Her walls were sometimes plastered and a stone coping placed on top. In most
instances, however, they were mortared or built as dry-stone walls with the beauty
of the stone fully exposed.

Retaining walls were usually clothed with trailing plants. Erigeron and other hardy
plants were allowed to colonise any holes in the wall that would support growth.
Walling particularly favoured south-facing borders raised on retaining walls, finding that 'the soft light coming from the south makes the effects produced on these
borders so much more pleasing than those facing north'.

Free-standing walls used to divide a garden were generally 24 to 27 inches tall,
a convenient sitting height. Often these walls had just the hint of a pier at the ends,
which protruded about 1 inch to give the walls a greater appearance of stability
and a better finish.

PLANTING FORM 'Winter is the biggest test of all when it comes to form in gardens;
nothing so reveals the weak points in our garden design.' [*Australian Home Beautiful*,
1929]

Much has already been said about the form of Edna Walling's gardens relying
heavily on architectural design. Naturally planting was very important in rein-
forcing this, and increased in importance the less formal a garden was. Evergreens
were used to great effect, very often in the opposite manner to that usually employed. For instance it was common, as it still is, to use evergreens as a backdrop

for deciduous planting, whereas Walling reversed this and often placed the deciduous trees in the rear to create a 'misty background'.

The general form of the planting was soft and rounded. Punctuation marks, however, were provided by columnar trees such as the Lombardy poplar, Roman cypress and the fastigiate birch. By using the subtleties of the green tonings combined with strong vertical elements, Walling was able to create wonderful feelings of solid and void, depth and perspective. Thus the often rigid architectural shapes of her gardens were softened, yet complemented, by the planting.

PLANTING TEXTURE 'When every other consideration is in its favour it is often found that a certain tree or shrub is not suitable because its "texture" is too fine or too coarse.' [*Australian Home Beautiful*, 1929]

For one who claimed to be bored by arranging planting schemes, Walling was a genius. She appreciated the fine texture of plants like leptospermums and loniceras that made them fade into the background, while the large-leaved plants such as rhododendrons and catalpas tended to leap out at the observer. The delicacy of her planting meant that the coarser-leaved varieties were used very sparingly. They were of course exploited when she wanted to achieve an effect of distance in a small garden by planting them in the foreground, with the finer varieties furthest from the viewer.

COLOUR IN PLANTING 'Osbert Sitwell has put into words an important truth — "one secret of the most beautiful gardens in the world — such creations as Villa d'Este, Caprarola, and the Villa Lante in Italy, or the Generaliffe in Spain — is that they show as few flowers as possible . . . green is the clue to creating a garden, and not the possession of all the hues in the rainbow". There is, of course, always the joy of the seasonal high spots provided by blossom and bulbs in spring, for example, hydrangeas in summer, autumn foliage, berries and chrysanthemums in the fall, but green is of paramount importance and the aforementioned colour effects only of secondary consideration; there is no escaping this fact. At certain times of the day there is such a diversity of tones among the greens in a well planted landscape garden, that there should be no feeling of monotony, even with no colour in the garden at the time.' [*Gardens in Australia*]

'The Long Walk' at Boortkoi, designed in 1937, is a feature of one of Edna Walling's most romantic surviving gardens

Walling adhered to this principle strongly. In her view, colour was of secondary importance to form and structure. She found the dazzling array of colour often seen in gardens far too confusing. If there were colours she did favour, they were the pale pastels and blue and white. She liked white flowers in particular for the very sensible reason that they could be seen and appreciated in the moonlight.

GROUPING PLANTS   'Only rarely should individual specimens be wholly isolated,' said Edna Walling in *Gardens in Australia*. She found that trees planted in lawns as specimens rarely achieved as good an effect as a copse of trees. At Sonning she planted a large copse of liquidambar. More generally she planted birch. At that time these were no ordinary groupings of trees. She scoured the nurseries to obtain multi-stemmed birch, and if these were not available she would plant two or even three in the same hole. Her aim was to achieve a more natural grouping. To do this she would sometimes fill a bucket with potatoes and hurl them over the ground. Where each potato landed a birch was planted. Now that these have had time to mature, the value of this method is greatly appreciated. 'Closely planted trees give glorious effects in moonlight, cool and restful shade in summer, and shelter and warmth in winter. Compare this with the specimen way — meticulous, unadventurous, and unattractive to the artist, the poet and to children', she said in *A Gardener's Log*.

In shrub beds plants were grouped so as to achieve gradual transitions from one form or colour — either flower or foliage — to another. Contrasting notes were used sparingly and even then were in harmony, rather than startling. Walling preferred to plant two or three or more of the same species together to avoid a spotting effect. She was often accused of overplanting, which she certainly practised. But the owner often forgot her instructions that the quick-growing 'nurse plants' were to be removed in favour of the slower-growing, more permanent ones. Herbaceous perennials and low-growing shrubs she found deficient in most gardens, but used widely in her own. The perennials were placed in the front of beds or often in a formal herbaceous border along the edge of a path. Very few annuals were used in a Walling garden, perennials being considered much more interesting and less labour-intensive.

A straight path, made less formal by the random nature of the birch copse at Mawarra

CHAPTER FOUR: THE LEGACIES OF EDNA WALLING

No other garden designer in Australia has influenced today's garden design idiom so much as Edna Walling. The much-acclaimed William Guilfoyle, although admired by many Melbourne people for giving them their Botanic Gardens, wrote little about his design work. In any case his was a form of design only available to the rich, as it needed a large area of land and much labour. Walling's various styles, on the other hand, were more accessible and feasible for most people. Her extensive writings introduced and cultivated a new interest and taste in garden design.

Many of the details that Walling used in her garden designs have become accepted and are popularly used — rock outcrops, gravel paths and stone walls. These details, illustrated in her books, are now part of the standard vocabulary of most landscape designers. Edna Walling was not always the first to use these design and construction elements in her gardens. But she was the first to give them a harmony and sense of proportion they had not enjoyed in Victorian and Edwardian times. Indeed she achieved a harmony in her gardens which is rarely surpassed.

The details, of course, varied according to the style of the garden. The cottage gardens at Mooroolbark had a rustic simplicity. Where foot tracks developed, they

'The Long Walk' and pergola at Boortkoi

were given an occasional sprinkling of Lilydale toppings; pergolas were constructed of young saplings across rough stone pillars, and rock outcrops were of the most natural type. They were the most unselfconscious of cottage gardens. But in the large city gardens the quality of the detailing needed to match the more refined architecture of the house. Dressed stone terraces were now covered with pergolas of dressed timber on circular or square stone columns. These were adequately 'toned down' by festoons of clematis and other climbers. Free-standing colonnades, flights of semi-circular stairs and rectangular pools could so easily have been stiff and formal.

The formal axial planning and refined detailing of the Ringland Anderson garden in Toorak is in marked contrast to the rustic cottages and gardens at Bickleigh Vale village

But the detailing of corners, edges and junctions was expertly handled to modify these more formal elements. Of course the erigeron, alyssum and other plants were encouraged to colonise the cracks between paving and walls, and helped to soften these harder structural elements. Regrettably, many of these details are now used in modern gardens without the sensitivity of Edna Walling.

Through her professional associates such as Ellis Stones and Glen Wilson, she passed on her ideas to an even wider public. These two men have often been seen as the creators of the new Australian garden design idiom. But the initial inspiration was undoubtedly Edna Walling's.

Her influence has been broader, however, than in garden design alone. Walling's ecological approach to planting and her interest in native plants have often been overlooked, yet these are lasting influences that have perhaps been most important of all.

Walling insisted on using plants which, although often exotics, were suited to the particular site conditions. Everywhere in her books is the evidence of this approach. Today it does not appear so significant, but in the 1920s in Australia it was revolutionary. Until then, the domestic gardening traditions of geometric beds stuffed with annuals, regimented rows of conifers and the ubiquitous standard roses were the order of the day. A garden which allowed the banksia rose to go unpruned and the foxgloves and columbines to seed in any desirable place was the exception rather than the rule. There had been, of course, other and earlier exceptions. In 1898 when describing to the owner of 'Dalvui' what was required in the 'Wilderness or Wild Garden' he was planning, Guilfoyle had said that 'A wild garden really means a picturesque confusion of plants and no formality of any kind'. And there were also the delightfully unpretentious cottage gardens which surrounded many a humble dwelling in both city and country.

Edna's ecological understanding is best seen in *The Australian Roadside*. As we have seen, Edna Walling advocated the sole use of indigenous plants on our highways in order to maintain and reinforce the regional character of a particular area. In her *Argus* article of 10 September 1937, she made a very strong plea for greater sympathy in designing and planting our highways. Speaking of the concept of roadside planting, she notes that there is 'a clear distinction between beautification or superficial decoration and fundamental organic roadside improvement'.

The pergola at Markdale has been modified, but the planting retains Wallings's touch

Such attitudes towards planting and design are now receiving wider recognition. Modern techniques of hydro-mulching with indigenous tree species would, most assuredly, have been applauded by Walling. So too would the ideas and techniques expressed in many books on native gardening — in particular the two excellent books by Betty Maloney and Jean Walker, *Designing Australian Bush Gardens* and *More About Bush Gardens* (1966 and 1967).

Edna Walling was one of the earliest advocates of native plants in gardens and parks as well as along highways. In the 1920s she was observing, identifying and collecting them in the bush — then propagating them in the nursery at Sonning. This interest grew until by the 1950s, she would only use native plants in her garden designs. Walling's early recognition of the beauty and usefulness of native plants did much to stimulate others to explore this field.

The source of the current Australian enthusiasm for native plants is complex and must certainly be linked with sentiments of nationalism. But the work of people like Edna Walling, who promoted the concept of ecological planting and fostered an awareness among the public of the beauty of native plants, also played an important part. It should not be forgotten, moreover, that she was responsible for popularising the use of many exotic plants in Victorian domestic gardens. The silver birch is the most obvious example. But so too did she focus attention on many of the less spectacular trees and shrubs at a time when the biggest, brightest and most elaborately variegated plants were enjoying a peak in popularity. The humble spiraeas, hawthorns, loniceras and single-flowering prunus were given a new status.

It is difficult to decide whether Walling's philosophy on buildings influenced anyone beyond Bickleigh Vale village. She was certainly known to many architects in

Melbourne, who must also have known of her work and writings. To Edna, houses should be simple but comfortable affairs. But above all, they should have an organic affinity with their site. Where possible, local materials should be used in the construction and the house should be 'extended' into the landscape by the use of walls, terraces, pergolas and the like. Walling was a great advocate of the use of pisé in house construction. The cottages she built at Bickleigh Vale village, as has been shown, were mostly of stone, rough sawn timber and timber shingles, with saplings

*One of a number of parallel
terraces at Mawarra*

cut from the site used for pergolas. When constructing rock walls she used a method also employed by Frank Lloyd Wright at his Taliesin studio and home. Formwork was built up to about 3 feet and filled with rocks, after which mortar was tamped into the cavities. Then the formwork was moved up for the next layer. 'Glencairn' at Bickleigh Vale was one cottage built in this way.

The conservation activities Edna Walling supported, including efforts to foster an interest in preserving Australia's roadside vegetation, have now largely been accepted by the public.

As a conservationist she was one of the earliest to use a combined ecological and visual base on which to prop her pleas for a more sensitive approach to landscape issues. This is nowhere better illustrated than in the chapters on 'Planting a Highway' and 'Roadside Ecology' in *The Australian Roadside*:

It is dangerous to embark on a tree planting project before thoroughly and sympathetically investigating the natural landscape resources of the district, and the wisdom of re-creating the natural scene is now so incontrovertible that we need no longer grope about when the matter of roadside planting presents itself.

Her village at Mooroolbark was the expression of a practical approach to conservation management in a residential environment. Although reluctant to join any conservation organisations, she supported and encouraged any cause she felt worthy.

She imparted something of this fighting spirit to many with whom she came into contact. Ellis Stones was not the least. His wranglings with the Melbourne and Metropolitan Board of Works in the 1950s and 1960s when they were putting many of Melbourne's small creeks into concrete drains would undoubtedly have received her support. Her early apprentice Gwynnyth Crouch later, as Gwynnyth Taylor, became a president of the Victorian National Parks Association and is still a keen and active supporter of planning and conservation issues.

But Walling's main contribution to the conservation cause must surely have been the new level of awareness she triggered off in the consciousness of many thousands of people through her articles and books. Her deep love of the bush, her delight in its flowers, its complex ecology and its subtle beauty are conveyed to the reader in the most captivating manner.

In her books, and particularly in *Cottage and Garden in Australia,* Walling tells an enchanting story of a life of simple and humble pleasure. In reality her busy professional life was quite different. It was a side of her that the reading public did not see. Those who were lucky were able to share the cottages, the village and the lifestyle of Bickleigh Vale. To many others Edna Walling's books were an inspiration and encouragement to adopt a simpler form of living. 'We seem to have lost the ability to create homely, comfortable and undoubtedly beautiful cottages — cottages which in their delightful simplicity express the kindly folk who built and inhabit them', she said in *Cottage and Garden in Australia.* It is little wonder that, with the current interest in alternative lifestyles, Walling's books are achieving new popularity and are in great demand.

As a garden designer Edna Walling was a master who dominated the scene in Victoria for forty years. Her legacy of gardens is gradually dwindling, but the few remaining are a memorial to her talent and her special idiom in garden design. Writing of the work of Gertrude Jekyll, William Robinson and Sir Edwin Lutyens, Derek Clifford has said:

it was neither a theatre, nor an ambulatory, nor a picture, nor a setting for a building, nor a poem, nor a demonstration of a philosophic principle, nor a scientific collection: It was in part all of these, but it was predominantly itself, a work of art in a kind unlike any other.

The same is true of Edna Walling's work. She introduced to Australia a totally new concept of garden design. The influences on her work are clear but, in adapting the ideas of others to the peculiarly Australian conditions, she gave to her gardens a unique and individual stamp.

If her surviving gardens were her only legacy, Walling could not, perhaps, claim such importance. But her influence goes far beyond them, as we have seen.

Edna Walling possessed a number of qualities which are relatively common, but in combination are extremely rare. Not only did she have a wonderful sense of design and a wide knowledge of plants, but she also had the capacity to write about her work and ideas in the most delightful and convincing way. Her commitment to sound conservation practices and the energy with which she pursued her goals remain, too, an inspiration to many.

Edna's photograph of the verandah at Sonning

APPENDIX I: SIGNIFICANT DATES

1896	Born 4 December
1911	Moved with family to New Zealand
1914	Moved with family to Melbourne, Australia
1916-17	Attended Burnley Horticultural College, Melbourne
1918-19	Worked as a jobbing gardener
1921	Built 'Sonning I'
1926	Commenced writing for *The Australian Home Beautiful*
1936	'Sonning I' destroyed by fire
	'Sonning II' commenced
1943	*Gardens in Australia* published
1947	*Cottage and Garden in Australia* published
1948	*A Gardener's Log* published
	Purchased East Point, Lorne
	Designed village at Mount Kembla
1949	Designed village at Port Pirie
1951	Shifted to 'The Barn'
1952	*The Australian Roadside* published
1967	Moved to 'Bendles', Buderim, Queensland
1973	Died 8 August

Foxgloves near the front door of Sonning I

APPENDIX II: PLANTS COMMONLY USED BY EDNA WALLING

Since Edna Walling used a continually growing and changing range of plants, it is not easy to provide a complete list. The species included are those most frequently referred to in her writings and shown on her drawings. Plants used in specialist gardens, such as those on the coast, are not listed here. Botanical names given are those currently in use; they are not necessarily the ones used in the Walling books. The common names of these plants have changed much less.

TREES FOR SHRUB BEDS

Acer campestre (Hedge Maple)
Acmena smithii (Lilly-pilly)
Anopterus glandulosus (Tasmanian Laurel)
Betula pendula 'Laciniata' (Swedish Birch)
Carpinus caroliniana (American Hornbeam)
Chamaecyparis lawsoniana 'Triomf van Boskoop'
Cotinus coggygria (European Smoke Tree)
Crataegus durobrivensis
C. phaenopyrum (Washington Thorn)
C. pubescens (Mexican Hawthorn)
C. crusgalli
C. tanacetifolia (Tansy-leaf Hawthorn)
Cupressus arizonica (Smooth Arizona Cypress)
Jacaranda mimosifolia (Jacaranda)

Lagerstroemia indica (Crepe Myrtle)
Malus 'Aldenhamensis' (Aldenham Purple Crab)
M. angustifolia (Violet-scented Crab)
M. 'Eleyi'
M. floribunda (Japanese Crab)
M. ioensis (Prairie Crab)
M. 'Sonningensis' (Sonning Crab)
M. sylvestris (Common Crab Apple)
Morus alba (White Mulberry)
Populus tremula (Aspen)
Prunus cerasifera 'Pissardii' (Purple-leaved Plum)
P. mume (Japanese Apricot)
P. spinosa 'Purpurea' (Purple-leaved Blackthorn)
Pyrus amygdaliformis

FASTIGIATE TREES FOR VERTICAL CONTRAST

Betula pendula 'Fastigiata' (Pyramid Birch)
Callitris glaucophylla (White Cypress Pine)
Carpinus betulus 'Fastigiata' (Fastigiate Hornbeam)
Cupressus sempervirens 'Gracilis' (Slender Italian Cypress)
C. torulosa 'Cashmeriana' (Bhutan Cypress)
Juniperus communis (Common Juniper)
Quercus robur fastigiata (Cypress Oak)
Ulmus carpinifolia sarniensis (Jersey or Wheatley Elm)

SPECIMEN TREES IN LAWNS

Platanus occidentalis (Buttonwood or American Sycamore)
Populus alba (White Poplar)
P. nigra italica (Lombardy Poplar)
Pyrus ussuriensis (Manchurian Pear)
Quercus rubra (Red Oak)
Zelkova serrata (Japanese Zelkova or Keaki)

TREES FOR COPSE PLANTING

Betula pendula (Silver Birch)
Leptospermum laevigatum (Coastal Tea-tree)
Liquidambar styraciflua (Sweet Gum)

PLANTS FOR WALLS, FENCES AND TRELLISES

Berberis x *stenophylla* (Rosemary Barberry)
Buddleja alternifolia (Fountain Buddleia)
B. salviifolia (Winter Buddleia)
Ceanothus x *edwardsii* (Edwards Ceanothus)
C. rigidus (Monterey Ceanothus)
C. x *vieitchianus*

Edna's 1927 plan for the conversion of the tennis court at Coombe Cottage. Regrettably, it was never built

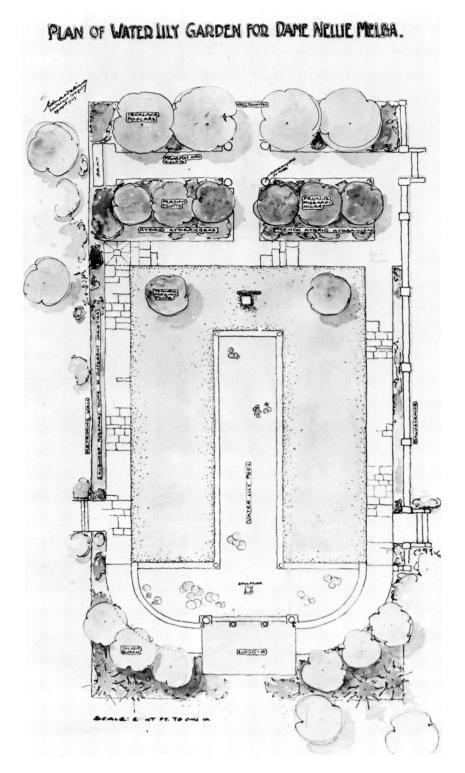

PLAN OF WATER LILY GARDEN FOR DAME NELLIE MELBA.

Chaenomeles speciosa 'Moerloosii' (a 'Japonica')
Cotoneaster franchetii (Franchet Cotoneaster)
C. simonsii (Simons Cotoneaster)
Escallonia x *rockii* cv. *freytheyi* (Frethey Escallonia)
Forsythia suspensa (Golden Bells)
Jasminum grandiflorum (Large-flowered Jasmine)
J. nudiflorum (Winter Jasmine)
Pyracantha sp. (Firethorns)

MEDIUM TO LARGE SHRUBS

Camellia sasanqua (Sasanqua or Apple-blossom Camellia)
Chimonanthus praecox (Allspice)
Choisya ternata (Mexican Orange-blossom)
Crataegus laevigata (Smith Hawthorn)
Cystisus x *praecox* (Warminster Broom)
Escallonia 'Edinensis'
Forsythia x *intermedia* 'Spectabilis' (Showy Golden Bells)
Jasminum nudiflorum (Winter Jasmine)
Kalmia latifolia (Mountain Laurel or Calico Bush)
Kolkwitzia amabilis (Chinese Beauty Bush)
Leptospermum lanigerum (Woolly Tea-tree)
L. rotundifolium (Round-leaf Tea-tree)
L. scoparium (Manuka)
Lonicera japonica (Japanese Honeysuckle)
Magnolia denudata (Yulan)
M. grandiflora (Laurel Magnolia or Bull Bay)
M. x *soulangeana* (Saucer Magnolia)
Olearia phlogopappa 'Coerulea' (Blue Dusty Daisy-bush)
Philadelphus mexicanus (Mexican Mock-orange)
Prostanthera ovalifolia (Oval-leaf Mint-bush)
Pyracantha crenulata (Nepal Firethorn)
Viburnum x *burkwoodii* (Burkwood Viburnum)
V. carlesii (Korean Viburnum)
V. farreri (Fragrant Viburnum)
V. tinus (Laurustinus)

SMALL SHRUBS

Abelia chinensis (Chinese Abelia)
Baeckea ramosissima (Rosy Heath-myrtle)
Berberis 'Rubrostilla'

A plan published with one of Edna's articles in Home Beautiful *as a guide to the owners of smaller suburban gardens*

B. thunbergii var. *atropurpurea* (Purple Japanese Barberry)
B. vulgaris 'Atropurpurea' (Purple-leaf Barberry)
Boronia muelleri (Tree or Forest Boronia)
Calytrix tetragona (Common Fringe-myrtle)
Ceanothus rigidus (Monterey Ceanothus)
Chaenomeles (Japonica)
Correa alba (White Correa)
Cytisus purpureus (Purple Broom)
Daphne odora alba (White Winter Daphne)
Erica sp. (Heaths)
Eriocephalus africanus (White Woolly-head)
Eriostemon myoporoides (Long-leaf Waxflower)
Grevillea confertifolia (Dense-leaf Grevillea)
Hebe sp. ('Veronica')
Hydrangea quercifolia (Oak-leaf Hydrangea)
Kalmia latifolia (Mountain Laurel or Calico Bush)
Lavandula sp. (Lavender)
Lithodora diffusa 'Heavenly Blue'
Micromyrtus ciliata (Heath-myrtle)
Pieris sp. (Pear-flower)
Plumbago auriculata (Cape Plumbago)
Rhododendron glaucophyllum
R. occidentale
Rhododendron sp. (Kurume azaleas)
Rosa sp. (Rose)
Spiraea sp. (May or Spiraeas)

LOW PLANTS FOR EDGING PATHS

Achillea millefolium (Milfoil or Yarrow)
Androsace lanuginosa
Anthemis aizoon
Arenaria montana (Mountain Sandwort)
Armeria maritima alpina (Alpine Thrift)
A. juniperifolia

Bellis rotundifolia
Brachyscome graminea (Grass-leaf Daisy)
B. multifida (Cut-leaf Daisy)
Erica x *darleyensis* (Darley Heath)
Erigeron karvinskianus (Babies' Tears)
Gaura lindheimeri
Geranium, alpine var.
Hypericum sp.
Lithodora diffusa 'Heavenly Blue'
Micromyrtus ciliata (Heath-myrtle)
Myosotis scorpioides (Water Forget-me-not)
Prunella grandiflora (Large-flowered Self-heal)
Raoulia tenuicaulis
Rosmarinus x *lavandulaceus* (Prostrate Rosemary)
Salvia azurea (Blue Sage)
Samolus repens (Creeping Brookweed)
Thymus serpyllum (Wild Thyme)
Veronica prostrata (Matted Speedwell)
Vinca minor (Lesser Periwinkle)

GROUND-COVERING PLANTS

Ajuga reptans (Bugle)
Brachyscome multifida (Cut-leaf Daisy)
Campanula sp. (Bell-flowers)
Cerastium tomentosum (Snow-in-summer)
Frankenia sp. (Sea-heaths)
Hypericum calycinum (Aaron's Beard)
Solenopsis auxillaris (Rock Isotome)
Nierembergia caerulia (Cup Flower)

FREE-GROWING HEDGES

Berberis sp. (Barberries)
Cotoneaster sp. (Cotoneasters)
Lonicera sp. (Woodbines or Honeysuckles)
Prostanthera sp. (Mintbushes)
Pyracantha sp. (Firethorns)

Spiraea sp. (May or Spiraeas)
Syringa sp. (Lilacs)
Vaccinium sp. (Whortleberries)
Viburnum sp. (Viburnums)
Weigela sp. (Weigelas)

CLIMBING PLANTS:

Clematis x *jackmanii* (Large-flowered Clematis)
C. montana (Anemone Clematis)
C. montana var. *rubens* (Pink Anemone
    Clematis)
Gelsemium sempervirens (Carolina Jessamine)
Hardenbergia comptoniana (W.A. Coral-pea)
Hedera helix 'Tricolor' (Three-coloured Ivy)
Muehlenbeckia complexa (Maidenhair Creeper
    or Pohuehue)
Rosa banksii (Banksia Rose)
Vitis vinifera 'Purpurea' (Teinturier Grape)
Wistaria sp. (Wistarias)

HERBACEOUS PERENNIALS

Achillea sp. (Milfoils)
Anchusa sp. (Alkanets)
Aster sp. (Asters)
Auricula sp.
Campanula sp. (Bell-flowers)
Delphinium sp. (Delphiniums)
Dianthus sp., esp. 'Mrs Sinkins' (Pinks)
Digitalis sp. (Foxgloves)

Osteospermum ecklonis (Daisy-of-the-Veldt)
Iris sp. (Irises)
Lupinus sp. (Lupins)
Penstemon sp. (Penstemons)
Primula sp. (Primulas)
Saxifraga sp. (Saxifrages)
Trachelium caeruleum
Verbascum sp. (Mulleins)

PLANTS FOR SMALL POTS:

Aethionema sp. (Rock-cresses)
Androsace lanuginosa
Anthemis aizoon
Campanula garganica
C. isophylla
Galanthus sp. (Snowdrops)
Narcissus bulbocodium (Hoop-petticoat
    Daffodil)

QUICK-GROWING NURSE PLANTS

Abelia sp. (Abelias)
Ceanothus sp. (Ceanothuses or Californian
    Lilacs)
Psoralea sp. (Scurf-peas)
Robinia pseudoacacia (False Acacia or Black
    Locust)
Spiraea sp. (May or Spiraeas)
Virgilia capensis (Cape Lilac)
Weigela sp. (Weigelas)

BIBLIOGRAPHY

GENERAL

Balmori, D., McGuire, D. and McPeck, E. *Beatrix Farrand's American Landscapes*. Sagapress, New York, 1985.

Barrett, Margaret (ed.). *The Edna Walling Book of Australian Garden Design*. Anne O'Donovan, Melbourne, 1980.

— *Edna Walling's Year—Ideas and Images from All Seasons*. Anne O'Donovan, Melbourne, 1990.

— *The Garden Magic of Edna Walling*. Anne O'Donovan, Melbourne, 1988.

Bligh, Beatrice. *Cherish the Earth*. Ure Smith, Sydney, 1973.

Bloomfield, Reginald. *The Formal Garden of England*. 1892. Reprint. Sagapress, New York, 1985.

Clifford, Derek. *A History of Garden Design*. Faber, London, 1962.

Dixon, Trisha and Churchill, Jennie. *Gardens in Time: In the Footsteps of Edna Walling*. Angus & Robertson, Sydney, 1988.

— *The Vision of Edna Walling*. Bloomings Books, Melbourne, 1998.

Fielden, Lorna. 'The Gardener's Warning'. The Author, Melbourne, n.d.

Hall, Barbara and Mather, Jenni. *Australian Women Photographers 1840–1960*. Greenhouse, Melbourne, 1986.

Jekyll, Francis. *Gertrude Jekyll*. Jonathan Cape, London, 1934.

Jekyll, Gertrude. *A Gardener's Testament*. Country Life, London, 1937.

— *Colour in the Flower Garden*. Country Life, London, 1908.

— *Home and Garden*. 1900. Reprint. Antique Collectors' Club, Woodbridge, 1982.

— *Old West Surrey*. Longmans Green, London, 1904.

— *Wall, Water, and Woodland Gardens*. 1901. Reprinted. Antique Collectors' Club, Woodbridge, 1982.

— *Wood and Garden*. 1899. Reprint. Antique Collectors' Club, Woodbridge, 1981.

— *The Making of a Garden*. An anthology compiled by Cherry Lewis. Antique Collectors' Club, Woodbridge, rev. ed. 1985.

Jekyll, G. And Hussey, C. *Garden Ornament*. 1918. Reprint. Antique Collectors' Club, Woodbridge, 1982.

Jekyll, G. And Weaver, Sir Lawrence. *Gardens for Small Country Houses*. 1912. Reprint. Antique Collectors' Club, Woodbridge, 1981.

Latreille, Anne. *The Natural Garden. Ellis Stones: His Life and Works*. Viking O'Neill and Penguin, Melbourne, 1990.

Lonie, Rachael. 'The Relationship of House to Garden Explored through the Work of Edna Walling.' Unpublished thesis, B. Arch., University of Sydney, 1990.

Massingham, Betty. *Miss Jekyll—Portrait of a Great Gardener*. David & Charles, London, 1966.

Robinson, W. *English Flower Garden*. 1883. Reprint. Sagapress, New York, 1984.

— *The Wild Garden*. 1870. Reprint of 5th ed. 1895. Timber Press, Portland, 1994.

Salon, Marlene. 'Beatrix Jones Farrand—Pioneer in Gilt-edged Gardens'. *Landscape Architecture*, January 1977, pp.69–77.

— 'Beatrix Farrand Landscape Gardener: Her Life and Work.' Unpublished thesis, M.L.A., University of California, Berkeley, 1976.

Stones, Ellis. *Australian Garden Design*. Macmillan, Melbourne, 1971.

Tanner, H. And Begg, J. *The Great Gardens of Australia*. Macmillan, Melbourne, 1976.

Watts, Peter. *Historic Gardens of Victoria*. Oxford University Press, Melbourne, 1983.

'Wilma'. 'A Career for Australian Girls: How to Earn a Living with Spade, Fork and Brains'. *Everylady's Journal*, 1 January 1927.

Wilson, Glen. *Landscaping with Australian Plants*. Nelson, Melbourne, 1975.

SELECTED WRITINGS OF EDNA WALLING

Books:

The Australian Roadside. 1952. Reprint. Pioneer Design Studio, Lilydale, 1985.

Cottage and Garden in Australia. Oxford University Press, Melbourne, 1947.

A Gardener's Log. 1948. New edition. Anne O'Donovan, Melbourne, 1985.

Gardens in Australia— Their Design and Care. 1943. New edition. Bloomings Books, Melbourne, 1999.

Letters to Garden Lovers. New Holland, Sydney, 2000.

On the Trail of Australian Wildflowers. Mulini Press, Canberra, 1984.

Articles:

Age. 24 March 1949.

'The Architecture of the Garden'. Centenary Gift Book, Melbourne, 1934.

Argus. 10 September 1937.

The Australia Handbook. 1939.

Edna checking the car at an overnight camp on the way to Horsham

Australian Home Beautiful. 12 January 1926; 12 February 1926; 12 March 1926; 12 April 1926;
12 May 1926; 7 June 1926; 5 July, 1926; 2 August 1926; 1 September 1926; 1 November 1926;
1 December 1926; 1 January 1927; 1 February 1927; 1 March 1927; 1 April 1927; 2 May 1927;
1 June 1927; 1 August 1927; 1 September 1927; 1 November 1927; 2 January 1928; 1 February
1928; 1 March 1928; 1 May 1928; 1 December 1928; 1 January 1929; 1 March 1929; 1 April 1929;
1 May 1929; 2 September 1929; 1 October 1929; 1 November 1929; 1 January 1930; 1 February
1930; 1 March 1930; 1 May 1930; 2 June 1930; 1 September 1930; 1 November 1930; 2 February
1931; 2 March 1931; 1 February 1932; 2 May 1932; 1 June 1932; 1 July 1932; 1 August 1932;
1 May 1933; 1 June 1933; 1 September 1933; 1 December 1933; 1 April 1934; 1 June 1934.

Australian House and Garden. October 1949.

Australian Woman's Mirror. 1925; 20 November 1928; 4 December 1928; 18 December 1928.

Croydon Mail. 16 December 1948; 1 December 1949.

Herald. 22 August 1955.

'Improving the Farm and Curing Erosion'. (ABC radio talk, 3 September 1951: MS in the
possession of the author).

South Australian Homes and Garden. 1 March 1939.

Walkabout. September 1950; 1 February 1951.

Note for 2002 reprint

Since the original publication of this book there have been numerous new books about Walling, reprints of her work and one of her manuscripts and a volume of her *Home Beautiful* articles have been published. This bibliography has been updated to include major new books only. In recent years the La Trobe Library, State Library of Victoria, has also established a significant Edna Walling Collection. It contains plans, drawings, manuscripts, photographs and other material. A large web site has also been established, by the Australian Broadcasting Corporation, at www.abc.net.au/walling/.

INDEX